FAVOR IN BUSINESS

*Inspiring Business Stories from Great
Entrepreneurs in American History*

SAUL FLORES JR.

WESTBOW
PRESS®
A DIVISION OF THOMAS NELSON
& ZONDERVAN

For more information on the author, visit www.saulflores.com.

WestBow Press books may be ordered through booksellers or by contacting:

WestBow Press
A Division of Thomas Nelson & Zondervan
1663 Liberty Drive
Bloomington, IN 47403
www.westbowpress.com
844-714-3454

Scripture taken from the King James Version of the Bible.

Scripture taken from the New King James Version® Copyright © 1982 by Thomas Nelson. Used by permission. All rights reserved.

Scripture quotations taken from The Holy Bible, New International Version® NIV® Copyright © 1973 1978 1984 2011 by Biblica, Inc. TM. Used by permission. All rights reserved worldwide.

Scripture taken from the World English Bible.

ISBN: 978-1-6642-8514-9 (sc)
ISBN: 978-1-6642-8515-6 (hc)
ISBN: 978-1-6642-8516-3 (e)

Library of Congress Control Number: 2022922197

Print information available on the last page.

WestBow Press rev. date: 12/12/2022

To my greatest mentor, my father, Saul Flores Sr.

His passion for Christ has been a consistent example of what takes place when a person falls in love with Jesus.

CONTENTS

ACKNOWLEDGMENTS

I give thanks to Jesus Christ. I thank Him for how He showers me with His love every day in a new way. He is my shoulder to lean on in times of trouble. He is my dearest friend and closest companion. I am extremely grateful for His loving kindness.

I also thank my constant cheerleader and encourager, Irma Flores. She has always been my greatest supporter. I couldn't have ever hoped for a greater wife and partner in this journey of life.

I thank my two beautiful daughters, Sarai Elizabeth Flores and Isabella Alicia Flores. They were willing to sacrifice family time in order to encourage me to finish this book.

Thank you to my daughter Sarai. She has been dependable help, on whom I've leaned when I needed guidance for this book. I'm very grateful for her contributions.

Thank you also to Cecily Paterson. She also has been a blessing in her counsel and contributions.

INTRODUCTION

God's favor played a vital role in the lives and work of many of the greatest Christian entrepreneurs in our nation's history. As a Christian and an entrepreneur, I was intrigued and inspired to discover more about their faith, dedication, and selfless giving as I wrote this book.

I was unaware of the magnitude of their giving or how God supernaturally prospered them because of their faithfulness. John D. Rockefeller, who, at the age of fifty-three, became America's first billionaire, spoke of his belief that making money was God's gift. I realized how God uses the gift of creating wealth to benefit His kingdom on earth.

Mary Kay Ash, the powerful, godly leader of the Mary Kay Cosmetics enterprise, received a dream from God to become a great ambassador of the gospel in the marketplace. Even though she went up against giant obstacles, she refused to allow her dream to die. She followed the Golden Rule as her guiding philosophy, similar to her inspiration, James Cash (J. C.) Penney. She not only prioritized her life as God first, family second, and career third, but she also encouraged her employees and sales force to do the same. God uses businesspeople in the marketplace to be a light that shines in darkness.

The unique stories in this book are backed by both in-depth research and scripture to verbalize the truth that we can never outgive God. God's Word promises to reward and bless those who pay tithes and give to His kingdom. God doesn't look at the amount we give; rather, He looks at the heart behind the giving and opens the storehouses from heaven upon the faithful.

Favor in Business is the compilation of decades of research, discovery, and prayer. I pray you find great encouragement and inspiration within these stories.

Chapter 1

ANOINTING WITH OIL

John Davison Rockefeller, 1839–1937

Think of giving not as a duty but as a privilege.

—John D. Rockefeller

For his eighth birthday, Johnny received the best present he could have imagined.

"Come this way, Johnny," his mother said, leading him outside.

Johnny followed her down the steps, out through the kitchen yard, and down to the henhouse. Johnny held his breath and hardly dared to hope. He loved their chickens so much. Could he really be getting …?

"Your very own turkey," his mother's voice broke into his thoughts, and Johnny smiled. She reached into the henhouse and brought out a large brown fowl with smooth, beautiful feathers and bright eyes. "She's a pedigree," his mother said proudly, "and she's yours."

Unable to say anything, Johnny took her from his mother's hands and cradled her in his arms.

For many nights afterward, Johnny was unable to sleep. Having his own turkey was a dream come true. He'd seen his mother look after the clutches of eggs while they waited to hatch, as well as the handfuls of coins she'd brought home from the market when she sold the young pullets and cockerels. He tossed and turned while visions of successful farming filled his mind. How many poults would his turkey have? And how much money would he make from her first clutch?

Over the next few months, Johnny took good care of his turkey and cleaned her roost faithfully. He diligently watched for signs of foxes and snakes, and he repaired the coop whenever he found anything that might cause harm. He looked for the fattest, juiciest grasshoppers he could find to supplement the feed he scattered twice a day, and he made sure she always had fresh, clean water.

Eventually, his little turkey began to lay. Johnny bounced with impatience and hovered anxiously while he counted the days until the emergence of the fluffy little brood. Much to his delight, five noisy, healthy poults were soon snuggled beneath his turkey's protective wings.

Oh boy, I'm going to be the richest kid in the whole county, Johnny thought while he calculated his profits. *If I sell them for twenty cents each, I'll have a whole dollar.* That was an enormous amount of money for someone his age in the mid-1800s.

When the five poults were old enough, young Johnny loaded them into a crate and set off to seek a buyer. After presenting the virtues and benefits of his stock to several local farmers, Johnny was thrilled when a neighbor agreed to buy all five. Johnny closed the deal with a handshake and shoved the dollar as deep as possible into his pocket.

With his money securely tucked away, the young entrepreneur sprinted excitedly down the long dusty lane and ran all the way home. He was rich! He could buy anything! A kaleidoscope of fantasies swirled through his head as his feet pounded the old dirt road. There were so many things he could buy—toys, candies, ice cream. Nothing was out of his reach. His mom was going to be so proud that her son was now a rich young man.

Johnny was breathing hard from excitement and exertion as he burst into the kitchen. "Ma, you won't believe it. I sold all five of my baby turkeys. I must be the richest kid in the whole county. Can you believe it, Ma?"

She shook his hand like an adult and grinned back at him. "I believe it, son; you can do anything you set your mind to complete. You're very smart. And you worked hard for this."

Johnny did a little dance around the kitchen. His happiness at the thought of all that money, just for him, was overwhelming.

"There is one thing I need you to realize, though," his mother said somberly.

Johnny stopped dancing. "What is it, Ma?"

"Well, son, not all of that money is yours."

Dumbfounded and a bit angry, Johnny looked at her. "But Ma, it *is* mine. I worked hard for it. How can it not be mine?"

"The Bible says that our money belongs to God," explained his mother. "All money belongs to God. He gave you the strength and health to make your first dollar, and now, He asks that you comply with His Word and return 10 percent to Him."

"But that's a whole dime, Ma! That's far too much." The fledgling businessman began to negotiate. "Can I just give Him a penny?"

"Now, son, I guarantee you that if you fulfill your obligation with God, you'll never regret it." His mom brought their well-used Bible to the table and turned to the book of Malachi. "'For I am the Lord, I change not.' That's from Malachi 3:6," she read. "And then, a little further on, 'Will a man rob God? Yet ye have robbed me.' If you look a few verses down, you see Malachi 3:10. 'Bring ye all the tithes into the storehouse, that there may be meat in mine house, and prove me now herewith, saith the Lord of hosts, if I will not open you the windows of heaven, and pour you out a blessing, that there shall not be room enough to receive it.'"

As she shut the Bible, Johnny was quiet as he thought about those words for a minute.

"I guess you're right, Ma. After all, I'll still be the richest kid in the county."

Johnny continued to raise healthy premium turkeys and faithfully gave 10 percent from each sale to the local Baptist church. In time, he became a prosperous young man and realized that his mom was right. He never regretted returning 10 percent of his income to God.

In 1855, Johnny turned sixteen and found a job as a bookkeeper for a local wholesale firm, Hewitt and Tuttle. As always, John demonstrated an excellent work ethic, starting at 6:30 a.m. and often working until 10:00 p.m., even though he was only earning four dollars a week. Jobs were tight, and John was unwilling to quit. But even though he was underpaid, he continued to give 10 percent of his earnings to the local Erie Street Baptist Church.

He believed and trusted that God would open a supernatural door of prosperity when the time was right. While he waited, John gave generously, almost fanatically. His gifts supported preachers, poor congregants, missionaries, and a school for the poor.

God honored his faith and actions. When Tuttle quit the firm, Hewitt offered half of the company to his hardworking bookkeeper, John. He accepted, of course, and more than doubled his pay. While John was proud of the achievement, he realized it was God who had arranged this door of opportunity, just as He had promised.

Under John's leadership, the company prospered, and by the time that John D. Rockefeller turned twenty-three, he was one of only a few young self-made millionaires in America.

John's generosity and willingness to give was something that stayed with him his entire life. He regularly gave over and above the standard 10 percent that his mom had taught him.

Later, John wrote,

> I have tithed (given ten percent of) every dollar God has entrusted to me. And I want to say, if I had not tithed the first dollar I made, I would not have tithed the first million dollars I made. Tell your readers to train their children to tithe, and they will grow up to be faithful stewards of the Lord" (Grant 2001).

John Rockefeller was very willing to use his money to help people in desperate situations. In 1865, a freed slave from Cincinnati heard of John's charitable giving and saw John as his only hope. It took some determination, but he was able to present his case to John. Without hesitation, John D. Rockefeller was able to help him buy his wife out of slavery.

At the age of fifty-three, Rockefeller became America's first billionaire. This gave him a level of wealth never seen before in the United States. Then John developed alopecia, which is an autoimmune disorder as well as a digestive disease. His body was in tremendous pain, and he lost all of his hair. The man with enough money to dine at the most prestigious restaurants in New York City could only swallow crackers and milk. He couldn't sleep or smile. It was as if the rest of his life were frozen in time.

The wealthiest man in America procured the best physicians in the world, but none was able to cure him. Gravely, they determined that John had only one more year to live.

John once woke in a state of great fear and panic. "I had a terrifying dream," he said later. "I was on the verge of leaving this body. Death was calling out to me, and I almost surrendered. But then I heard a voice. The voice of an angel said, 'Your mission on earth is unfinished. Do not worry about whether or not you will die. You will live. You are a man with a great destiny to fulfill on earth. Remember this, and don't forget it. When you leave this earth, you will leave your riches behind'" (Tan 1998).

This dream made a notable impact on John D. Rockefeller. At this point, his total worth was approximately $900 million, and the dream rekindled his desire to give his money away to benefit humanity. Finding new and radical ways to be generous, John gave away $540 million.

Some people considered this act foolish or irrational, but John realized something. Not only could he not outgive God, but he could not afford to lose sight of the fact that the Most High God allowed him to have money to give in the first place.

John said, "It has seemed as if I was favored and got increases because the Lord knew that I was going to turn around and give it back" (Mike 2018).

As soon as he resumed his extravagant giving, Rockefeller's company, Standard Oil, began to show astonishing profits. Even though he gave away the bulk of his fortune, he gained even more wealth. Amazingly, the moment he began to give back a portion of all that he earned, his body's chemistry was altered so significantly that he recovered. It looked as if he would die at fifty-three, but he lived to be ninety-eight.

John D. Rockefeller was anointed for business and empowered to gain wealth because God knew that he would be willing to give the money back to help others.

"I believe the power of making money is a gift of God," John said later. "I believe it is my duty to go on making money and still more money, and to dispose of the money I make for the good of my fellow man according to the dictates of my conscience" (Grant 2001).

One of the biggest impacts John D. Rockefeller made with his money was in establishing the Giving Pledge, which challenges wealthy individuals to give back at least half of their wealth, if not during their lifetimes, then after their deaths.

Chapter 2

CLEANLINESS IS GODLINESS

William Colgate, 1783–1857

The only spiritual light in the world comes through Jesus Christ and the inspired Book; redemption and forgiveness of sin alone through Christ. Without His presence and the teachings of the Bible, we would be enshrouded in moral darkness and despair.

—Samuel Colgate (son of William Colgate)

Bam! Bam! Bam!

The loud knocking woke up young William. Who could be pounding on the door at this time of night? The boy stumbled out of bed, wrapping a blanket around his shoulders. Winter nights in England were cold. The wind managed to creep through the cracks and fill the farmhouse.

"Who is it?" William asked when he reached the hallway. His eyes adjusted to the light of the torch held by his father as he stood by the unopened front door. His father's face was firmly set, and William bit his bottom lip until he felt the metallic taste of his own blood.

A knock like this past midnight could only mean trouble, and it felt like danger had been building over the past few months. His father's beliefs about American freedom were radical, and he did not keep them to himself. Unfortunately for him, the government officials didn't like to be challenged during a time of war.

William's mind raced. Perhaps they would arrest his father, and William would never see him again. He blinked in the half light. At the age of twelve and as the eldest child, he would become the man of the house.

He put out his hand to touch his father's arm. "Should you open the door?" he asked. "It might be safer to keep it shut."

His father looked at him with a reproving smile. "Son," he said, "never be afraid to stand up for what you believe." He turned the doorknob, and the door swung open.

"Mr. Colgate, sir?" A single figure in a heavy overcoat stood at the door. William breathed a quiet sigh of relief. There were no guards—only one young man who looked damp and cold. "I have an important message for you," he said.

William's father invited him inside. He found some bread and tea and told William to stoke the fire so their guest would be warm. Then they sat down together to talk.

"The prime minister is worried for you. He has sent me to warn you," the man said. "If you keep on talking against the king, saying that Americans should have rights, then you will be arrested. Who can say what would happen to you then?" He paused and looked toward William. "And your family."

William's father's eyes drooped, but his mouth was set in a determined line. "Prime Minister Pitt is a good man and has always been a friend to me," he told the young messenger. "You can tell him not to worry. We will remove ourselves from the danger. The time for change here in England is not now. But perhaps God shall use our family to have some good effect in another part of the world."

William's eyes widened. They were leaving England? But where would they go? And what would they do if they no longer had their farm to work?

The next morning, his father broke the news to the rest of the family. Opening the Bible, he read the words of Jacob:

> And Jacob vowed a vow, saying, If God will be with me,
> and will keep me in this way that I go, and will give me
> bread to eat, and raiment to put on, So that I come again

to my father's house in peace; then shall the Lord be my
God: And this stone, which I have set for a pillar, shall
be God's house: and of all that thou shalt give me I will
surely give the tenth unto thee. (Genesis 28:20–22 KJV)

"God will be with us," said his father, "wherever we go."

The family boarded a ship headed for Baltimore in America. The voyage
was long, and as William looked out to the blue horizon, he pondered his
future. His father had talked about finding a farm when they arrived, but
he wasn't sure the farming life was for him. America was supposed to be
the land of opportunity, wasn't it? Perhaps there would be something else
he could make his own.

He found his "something else" when his father branched out from
farming their new property in Maryland and began manufacturing soap
and candles. William liked the idea of creating something new, and he
watched eagerly as his father worked with his partner to create these
products from scratch.

Unfortunately, the partnership was unsuccessful. It dissolved after
just two years, and his father went back to farming. At nineteen, William
decided to keep on with soap. "I'll go into business on my own," he told
his family.

Regrettably, this business also failed within a year. William was
disappointed, but he wasn't giving up. "I'll try again in New York City!"
he decided.

It was a long trip, and as William traveled on a canal boat, he talked
to the captain.

"Where are you heading, son?" the old man asked.

"I'm going to New York City to make soap," William replied.

"Soap, huh?" The captain looked at him through squinted eyes. "You're
a smart kid. You know, someone will soon be the leading soap maker in
New York. That guy could be you." He scratched his chin. "Let me give you
some advice. Make a quality soap. Give a full, honest pound. And never
lose sight of the fact that the soap you make has been given to you by God.
Honor Him by sharing what you earn. Begin by tithing all you receive."

The words stuck with William, and as he traveled, the verses from
Genesis that his father had read when they were leaving England also came

back to him. Jacob's vow had been about that very thing—giving back to God. What was it? A tenth of everything? He opened his Bible and read it again: "And of all that thou shalt give me I will surely give the tenth unto thee" (Genesis 28:22b KJV).

In his heart, he felt challenged. God had given him these opportunities. It was God who created every ingredient that went into the soap he loved to make. If he had been given so much, why would he not give God first place in his life and give back a tenth of his profits? He decided to tithe from the very first dollar he earned.

William Colgate and Company set up on Dutch Street in Manhattan in 1806, making and selling soap and candles. It was a success from the beginning, and as the company grew, William insisted on continuing to give back to God.

"Open a special account for the money for the Lord's work," he told his accountants. At first, he gave 10 percent of his profits, but later, it increased to 20 percent, then 30 percent, and eventually, up to half of his personal income.

William had built his business on biblical principles, and it became clear that God was directing his path as he became one of the most prosperous businessmen in New York City. In fact, it seemed the more money he gave to God, the more prosperous he became. God was making good on the promise He had made in Malachi 3:10 (NIV) to people who pay their tithes: He threw "open the floodgates of heaven and pour out so much blessing that there will not be room enough to store it." William was the soap king of New York City.

William matured in his Christian faith and lived with a passionate desire to help missionaries and charitable works. He was a deacon in his Baptist church on Oliver Street and gave money to support overseas missions. William helped found the American and Foreign Bible Society and was a generous giver to Madison University and Theological Seminary (renamed Colgate University in 1890).

As the business grew, William's sons became involved in the Colgate company. They were all generous, biblically minded, and good employers.

William Colgate died in March 1856, but his name is spoken daily around the world as people use his soap, toothpaste, and detergents. Colgate-Palmolive is globally known and loved, with products that almost everyone would recognize. In 2020, it had an annual sales revenue of over $16 billion. It is amazing what can happen when a young apprentice follows his dream, works hard, and acknowledges God in all he does.

William Colgate's desire to help people founded a legacy that continues to transform lives around the globe. From being the son of an outspoken farmer who had to flee for his life, William became a prosperous, influential businessman who continues to make a difference in the lives of generations of people due to his generosity.

Chapter 3

KETCHUP EMPIRE

Henry J. Heinz, 1844–1919

To do a common thing uncommonly well brings success.
—Henry J. Heinz

It was the headline in the newspaper that was the last straw: "Trio in a Pickle!" it shouted to the world (Lukas 2003), almost as if bankruptcy and failure were comical and entertaining. The headline felt like a personal insult to Henry. Ashamed and depressed at the collapse of his business, he had taken to his bed for several months.

"Will you come downstairs for Christmas dinner?" his wife implored.

He couldn't bring himself to celebrate. There was no point; there was no money for presents for the children. He could not stand to see the disappointment in their eyes. At the age of thirty-one, Henry Heinz was defeated. And he had no idea when—or how—he could ever rise again.

Depression had a firm hold of Henry's heart; he remained isolated in his bedroom for months. He thought back to better days, days filled with optimism and hope in his youth. He reminisced on the scents of his family garden, which had fresh produce year-round. The garden had provided more than enough food to feed his parents and many siblings.

One day, after picking all the vegetables from their garden, his mom told him to take the wheelbarrow into town and sell the produce their family would not eat.

"Everything that's left over?" asked Henry.

"Everything," said his mother. "We really need the money."

Henry set off that afternoon, maneuvering the unwieldy wheelbarrow as best he could. *Market time is over for the day*, he thought. *So what is the best way to sell this wheelbarrow full of produce?* He wanted to profit as much as possible for his parents.

"Door to door," he said to himself. "I'll start with my German neighbors."

"*Guten tag, fraulein.* Good day, ma'am," he said as he approached a woman he knew from the Lutheran church. "*Wie gehts?* How are you? I have the best fresh beans today. Would you like some?"

The Heinz family produce was not hard to sell in his neighborhood, and Henry was confident in the quality of his vegetables. Soon, he and his wheelbarrow were a regular feature in town, turning up in the afternoons with vegetables and fruit of all kinds—and, even better, sauces, like ketchup. Henry had begun making sauces himself from the age of nine, using his mother's old recipes that she had brought from Germany.

"How do I know they are fresh?" a customer asked him one day. "The horseradish I bought last week was bland and bitter."

"Well, where did you get it?" asked Henry.

"The grocery store."

"My horseradish is different," he said, holding up a glass jar. "When it is packed in glass, you can see what you're getting. Only the best quality from me."

The idea of using a clear glass jar, rather than a can, was revolutionary. Henry instinctually found solutions to problems he saw in selling produce.

As a result, he was able to sell more produce than his competitors. Every afternoon, he would bring back money to his parents from his profits. His father was impressed by Henry's work ethic and how he continued to honor them and share his profits.

"This is very good, my son," he said. "Since you have proven you are hardworking, we will give you more responsibility."

By the age of ten, Henry found himself the owner of nearly an acre of land, given to him by his parents. Two years later, he was growing vegetables on just under three acres, working hard every single day to produce quality crops and sell them. He graduated from the wobbly wheelbarrow to a horse and cart, which made transportation easier.

It was not, however, what his mother wanted. "The Lutheran school is a wonderful choice for a boy such as yourself," she frequently told Henry. "The Lord wants you to become a Lutheran priest. I'm sure of it."

Henry was not so sure. While he had his mother's faith in God, he also had a definite attraction to business.

Henry wanted his mom to see signs for a different calling on his life. Even in high school, his small vegetable and pickle business had grown so much that he was hiring people to keep up with demand. His produce was heavily stocked in the local grocer's shop. A farmer's yearly salary in the 1860s was $400. At the age of seventeen, he made over $2,000 from his garden in one summer.

Henry felt strongly that his true calling was to be a businessman so he could help others through giving. He worked hard and was able to pay his own way through business school.

In 1869, Henry found that a friend of his, Clarence Noble, was seeking a partner to form a new company. Clarence was looking to go into business selling horseradish, pickles, and other prepackaged foods. This could not be a coincidence. They decided to launch this new venture together.

The new company initially performed well; Henry found himself incredibly busy. They invested heavily in horses and carts for deliveries. Although the horses helped the company operate more efficiently, it also radically increased overhead expenses for the young business. With the backing of the bank, however, they continued to hope for a bright future.

In 1875, everything changed: a financial crisis that paralyzed the entire banking system of America. Heinz & Noble became collateral damage. The company was growing and depended on financing from the bank for its continued expansion. Additionally, the price of horseradish was dropping everywhere. Heinz & Noble was forced to file bankruptcy. The property was sold, and the business closed permanently.

Henry Heinz and his family were left with nothing, and this shattered Henry. He was so discouraged by this business failure that he fell victim to months of dark depression. Although he was deeply depressed, he was also burdened by the thought of not being able to pay his debtors.

"As bankrupt, I may not have any legal obligation to pay my debts, but it is my moral duty to pay them, nonetheless," he told his wife.

As a stickler for accurate records, he kept a Moral Obligation book of every single penny he owed. He would not be at peace until he had paid it all back.

One day, while Henry was alone in his room and still struggling to escape the grasp of depression, there was a knock on the door.

"Henry," his wife said gently through the door, "your mother is here."

Henry gathered his thoughts, straightened his clothes, and went into the living room to see his mother.

"Henry, *liebling.*" She greeted him with her usual loving voice. "Here are all my savings." She handed over a large bag with cash. "I believe in you with every fiber of my being. You are my son, and I love you."

"No, Mom, I can't let you do this," Henry interjected.

"Listen to me! You are a talented and wise businessman. I have realized that running a business is your calling. I know you will be successful. Do not give up on your goal! We should start a new company—a family-owned company. I will own the shares, but you'll run the business. Surely, we will succeed. God is with us!"

Heinz was back in business. With his mother's investment and the family behind him, he worked as hard as ever to get ketchup, pickles, and sauces back on the shelves in grocery stores. It took him five years to pay all the debts he owed. In the meantime, the company did well, and soon, Henry was back in position to be the legal owner.

The family company grew quickly. It didn't take long before Heinz tomato ketchup became wildly popular, made according to Henry's mother's recipe from Germany. Again, Henry made sure that glass bottles showed off the product's freshness.

Henry bought more factories and employed more people for his expanding business. At this time, his Christian virtues began to differentiate him from other factory owners. Henry believed deeply in going to great lengths to care for his staff and provide excellent facilities for them. Every factory he owned had a gym and swimming pool for employees to use. He also provided free health care, dental care, life insurance, and educational facilities. These were unprecedented employee benefits.

Giving his employees great benefits and employee breaks seemed unbusinesslike. After all, when his employees weren't working, Henry wasn't making a profit. But Henry took a different perspective: he was doing good for those he cared for. If he was going to take his Christian principle of loving your neighbor seriously, he had better start with his nearest neighbors. As it turned out, Henry developed a loyal, hardworking workforce. Jobs were hard to get at Heinz factories because no one ever wanted to leave!

In 1919, when Henry Heinz died of pneumonia at the age of seventy-five, he left behind an extraordinary business but also an important legacy of faith. The first line of his will read:

> I am looking forward to the time when my earthly career shall end. I desire to set forth, at the very beginning of this my Will, as the most important item in it, my confession of my faith in Jesus Christ as my Saviour forever. (Leigh 2013)

Henry consistently proved his faith in God throughout his life. He was involved in his local church by teaching Sunday school and supporting church projects with his finances. He also took mission trips to Japan, China, and Korea to testify to those who did not know the Lord. He had a passion for giving and helping people who were in need. Those who knew him believed that his life reflected Jesus's teachings.

The advice that Henry once gave to a young entrepreneur was a summary of his life philosophy: "Make all you can honestly, save all you can prudently, give all you can wisely" (Carnegie Medal of Philanthropy 2007). Henry's life was a demonstration of God's promise:

> Give, and it will be given to you. A good measure, pressed down, shaken together and running over, will be poured into your lap. For with the measure you use, it will be measured to you. (Luke 6:38 NIV)

Henry was a faithful steward in giving, so the Lord saw fit to prosper and bless Henry Heinz throughout his life.

Chapter 4

IT'S THE REAL THING

Asa Griggs Candler, 1851–1929

Asa saw his personal wealth as a divine trust to be used to the benefit of humanity.

—Kathryn Kemp, biographer

"Climb on, Asa!" called his brother. "Get on the cart. We're ready to go."

Eleven-year-old Asa stuffed his last bite of breakfast into his mouth and raced out the kitchen door to where his older brother was waiting at the gate to their farm.

"I want to sit on the top," Asa said.

His brother had stretched a canvas cover over the load of corn that filled the cart tray. Asa enjoyed sitting high above the large wooden wheels to see the world go by.

"I don't care where you put yourself," his brother said impatiently. "Just make it quick. We have to go if we're going to get to the market and sell all this corn."

"I'm *ready*," sang out Asa excitedly, climbing up and perching himself on top of the load. "Let's go!"

The trip to town took the boys, with their horse and cart, across the fields of their farm.

"It's bumpy!" called Asa's brother. "Hang on tight."

"I'm fine," replied Asa, annoyed at being treated as though he was younger than his age. As the eighth child in a family of eleven children, there was always someone bossing him around. He constantly had to speak up for himself, or he'd be drowned out.

"No, really," said his brother, jiggling around at the front, "hold on!"

"I'm fi—" began Asa. But the cart hit a big bump, and Asa went tumbling over before hitting the ground with a thump. He heard a squeal and a crunch, and then everything went black.

When Asa woke up, his mother's face, hovering in front of him, seemed blurry.

"What happened?" he asked, but she put her finger to her lips.

"Shhh. Don't talk. Just rest." She put her hands up to his face. "My poor baby. It's a miracle you're still here. God has saved you for a purpose."

Not only had Asa fallen from the cart—which would have been enough to cause serious injury—but his older brother had been unable to stop, and the wheel had run over his head. Recovery was slow, and Asa was left with regular migraines, deafness in one ear, and vision problems that would affect him for the rest of his life (Kemp 2002, 10).

The accident also left him with the deep, unshakeable belief that God had saved him for great things. What they were, he didn't know—yet. For now, he just had to get better, and get on with being a child in a big family in tough times.

Asa's father had been a successful farmer and retailer, and he was known in his community for being honest and upright. However, the American Civil War was about to break out, and when it did, income became difficult for the large Candler family. None of the children could go to school during the war, and his mother struggled to keep food on the table. Asa learned to work hard, just like every child in his family, but his chance to help make some money came when he heard a noise coming from the chicken coop under the house.

"What is it, Asa?" his mother asked. "A fox?"

"I'll go and find out," brave Asa said.

Asa crept downstairs to discover that a mink had gotten in with the hens and was trying to eat them. He chased it out and through the yard until he finally caught it—with his bare hands.

"It bit you," cried his sister as he came, triumphantly, back into the kitchen.

Asa rubbed his bleeding arm. "Yes, but I got it."

Mink pelts were valuable, and young Asa saw an opportunity. He managed to persuade a peddler to take it with him to Atlanta to see if he could sell it.

"I might get a whole quarter for it," he told his mother.

He was over the moon when the peddler came back with not just a quarter but a silver dollar for him. Asa figured that if there had been one mink, there must be more. His window of opportunity suddenly seemed bigger, so he set up a small but thriving business, hunting the animals and selling their pelts.

When Asa was old enough to go to college, he had vague thoughts about medical school but quickly decided he'd rather earn some money right away.

"You should go to college," his father told him. "Make something of yourself."

But Asa, who had developed the habit of having his voice heard, told his dad that he would go later. "For now, I need to learn everything I can by working," he said.

Asa started out in an apprentice to a pharmacist for a year and did well, but then his father passed away. Returning home, he spent some time sorting out the farm and providing for his mother. Life, as he knew it, was changing, and he was at a crossroads. It was time for him to make a serious commitment to God.

Asa's mother was the champion of the family's Christian faith. She had taken the children to church, prayed with them at night, and encouraged them to sing and play hymns together. She had also taught her children the importance of tithing, and Asa embraced this teaching throughout his life. Now, with the death of her husband, Asa's mother clung to her faith as never before, and Asa was moved. He formally joined the Methodist Church, and his faith became a passionate driving force in his life.

In 1873, with just $1.75 in his pocket, Asa Candler decided to move to Atlanta. He found a job with a pharmacist, who happened to have a beautiful daughter named Lucy. Asa brought his farming work ethic with him to the drugstore, as well as his ability to spot opportunities. His boss, however, was not impressed with Asa's pursuit of Lucy. So Asa eventually ventured out to establish a business of his own.

Again, doing something of which others disapproved, Asa secretly married Lucy four years later, and they had their first child, Howard, soon after. Working as a pharmacist did not bring Asa the success for which he had hoped, even though he worked hard. There were also more and more mouths to feed at home, with four sons and a daughter being born to them.

There must be an opportunity out there that no one else has spotted, he figured. Perhaps he could focus on patent medicines or concoctions that used a secret recipe unknown to other drugstore owners. He bought a few patents for different medicines, but nothing took off the way he hoped. He didn't know it, but what he was waiting for was already being made right there in Atlanta, Georgia.

John (Doc) Pemberton was an Atlanta pharmacist who had invented a soda that he claimed had medicinal benefits. Unfortunately, he didn't know how to market it or how to get other people to invest in it.

At first, Asa didn't appear interested when he heard about Pemberton's drink. Regardless, he watched the opportunity carefully to see what might come of this new beverage. Finally, when the moment was right, he bought the secret recipe for $2,300, becoming the sole owner of it in 1891, and the drink that would become Coca-Cola was his.

At this point, Asa's skills and work ethic came together. It was through advertising that Coca-Cola became successful. Asa knew that he needed a national audience for his drink, so he promoted it everywhere, with everything he could possibly think of—souvenir fans, calendars, clocks, and all sorts of marketing products. Posters of stylish young women drinking Coke were plastered around the country.

He was the first national entrepreneur to use celebrities to market his product. He even gave away thousands of coupons for a free glass of Coca-Cola, figuring that if customers could try this new taste for free, they'd fall in love with it and want to drink it again.

The key to Asa's product was a *secret ingredient* that no one else knew. Asa told no one how to make it, and he never wrote it down. He and his colleague memorized the formula so that it could never be stolen or copied.

There were rumors that Coca-Cola contained cocaine,[1] but by 1920, Asa had won a battle with the Food and Drug Administration. Coca-Cola was safe to drink, and it made him a millionaire. Demand increased, and the business grew so much that when Asa sold it in 1919, he made $25 million.

---

[1]   Coca-Cola did, in fact, contain cocaine when it was first manufactured. At the time, however, cocaine's negative properties were not known. This ingredient was gradually reduced and then taken out altogether.

In recent years, Coke has been sold in over two hundred countries and is the largest manufacturer, distributor, and marketer of nonalcoholic drink concentrates in the world. It makes over $33 billion in revenue and has eighty thousand employees—all because of young Asa Candler and his cleverness and determined work ethic.

Asa's Christian faith and how it showed up in his daily life was most important to him. When he wrote to his son at college later in life, his advice was, "Live so that it will not be needful for you to tell people you are religious, but in your life, constantly exhibit Christ" (Adams 2012, 55). Asa exhibited Christ as he shared his wealth and made huge donations to the Methodist Church, Emory University, and the city of Atlanta. He gave funds to build Wesley Memorial Hospital, which grew to become one of the top hospitals in America. The hospital was later renamed Emory University Hospital, and it continues to bless and heal families to this very day.

He lived by the idea that his personal wealth was a divine trust to be used for the benefit of humanity and that everyone should do what he or she could for the common good. It was this that pushed him to become mayor of Atlanta in 1916. He believed in serving and helping his community.

In his last years, Asa gave his entire fortune to Emory University, leaving only enough for himself to live on. The $7 million in donations to Emory was extremely beneficial to the young university. Due to his giving, the Candler School of Theology was named in honor of his family.

Asa died in 1929, a full sixty-seven years after the accident that should have killed him as a boy. God did save him for a purpose. He gave Asa the opportunities to be successful *and* generous, and Asa made the most of this opportunity.

Chapter 5

NOTHING IS BETTER FOR THEE THAN ME

Henry Parsons Crowell, 1855–1944

Take your time. Think it through. Find the will of God.
—Henry Parsons Crowell

The coughing was getting worse; it was not only during the night now. His father coughed and gasped for air all day. Nine-year-old Henry watched his mother, white-faced and anxious, as she wiped her husband's brow and tried to help him get slightly more comfortable.

Henry observed the doctor, grave and serious, listening to his father's chest and taking his pulse. Henry was afraid. *Tuberculosis.* The word was whispered between them at first, and then, as his father became weaker and sicker, it was spoken aloud.

"Henry, we must prepare ourselves," said his mother one day, with tears in her eyes. She folded him into her arms. "Father is getting worse, and there is nothing the doctors can do for him."

Henry was devastated. When the sad day of his father's funeral finally came around, and they had to say their final goodbyes, Henry buried his head in his mother's chest. He would have to be strong for her now. She needed him.

It was not until a few years later that Henry began to suspect symptoms of his own. His fear of tuberculosis returned. Surely, both he and his father would not be taken by the same disease.

The doctor examined him thoroughly, and then sat him and his mother down to give his diagnosis. "I know this is a lot to take in, young man," he said, leaning back in his chair, "but unless you do something now, you probably will tuberculosis in the next few years."

Henry knew what the doctor's words meant. He would die young, unless God miraculously spared him.

Henry's mother's eyes widened. "Doctor, there must be something you can do!"

"There's nothing *I* can do." The doctor's voice was firm. "But there's something *he* can do." He turned to Henry and spoke hesitantly. "Living here in Cleveland, Ohio, is not good for your health. Leave your home, young man, and go west. Live outdoors, away from the city. Breathe the good, clean air, and let your lungs recuperate. Don't take the chance that you might die of the same disease that killed your father."

"How long will it take for Henry to be well?" asked his mother.

The doctor considered for a moment. "Seven years. He'll need to be away in the West for seven years."

Henry's head was spinning. Leave his mother? His family? Seven years would mean he wouldn't be able to go to Yale. He wouldn't even graduate high school! This diagnosis was a crushing blow to his dreams. "I don't know if I can do this," he said to his mother.

She looked at him with tears in her eyes. "It's your only hope." Although she loved her son profoundly, she realized this sacrifice was necessary. She couldn't bear the thought of losing her son to the same disease that had taken her husband to an early grave.

After the loss of his father, Henry put his faith in Christ for strength. The family had always attended church, and Henry developed a strong relationship with God after his father's death. After hearing a sermon about being a witness by the famous preacher D. L. Moody, Henry made a commitment to God regarding his desire to be in business.

"I can't be a preacher," he prayed, "but I can be a good businessman. God, if you will let me make money, I will use it in your service." Henry's bargain was that if God allowed him to prosper, Henry would keep his own name out of it.

As Henry traveled in the western states, with no education or training, he had to have business savvy to succeed. He bred and traded horses successfully throughout this season in his life. After seven years, he was happily declared cured of tuberculosis. Now was the time to go home and pray for the business that was right for him.

"Henry, I have an idea for you," his uncle said one day. "There's a rundown oat mill for sale, out of Akron, Ohio."

"Why are they selling?"

"It's had two previous owners, and they didn't make a profit. But one of them filed a trademark to go with the oats they sold—the first-ever trademark for cereal. By filing the trademark, no one else will be able to use the logo on their packages."

"What's the trademark?" Henry asked.

"It's the figure of a man in Quaker clothes."

"Quakers," pondered Henry. "People think of good value and honesty when they think of Quakers."

"You should investigate it, at least," his uncle said.

Henry bought the Quaker mill in 1881, when oats were only fed to horses. Henry had a great task in front of him to educate Americans about the benefits of oat cereal. Selling the oats proved to be a challenge. The large bags of oats just weren't selling. His business was struggling.

"Lord, show me what to do," he prayed.

Soon, the Lord answered him through a revelation. Oats had always been sold in bulk, sitting in large sacks and containers on the store floors. Sometimes, rats or insects got into the oats and contaminated them. Therefore, people did not consider buying them as food for breakfast.

Henry's idea was simple but revolutionary. He would sell the oats in smaller quantities, packaged in small boxes. As a bonus, the boxes were perfect for advertising the benefits of oats as breakfast food!

He decided to get someone else to take care of the day-to-day operations of the mill, and he focused entirely on getting his cereal onto the shelves of grocery stores and, from there, onto the breakfast tables of America.

To his delight, his idea worked. Demand for Quaker Oats soared. Even during the 1893 depression, while businesses went bankrupt or were cutting back, Quaker Oats was thriving. Henry had labeled his oats as an affordable, nutritious alternative for families to eat in tough times. People purchased oats instead of more expensive foods, like beef. He embraced advertising and got celebrities to endorse his cereals.

"Why so much advertising?" people asked Henry. "Why not just get a sales team to convince store owners to stock your product?"

His reason was simple. "Direct advertising to housewives does a better job."

By advertising straight to the women who purchased his product, he discovered that they would ask their grocer to stock Quaker Oats. He didn't need to pay a sales force. The product would find its own way into the stores by customer demand.

Throughout their lives, the Crowell family was known not only for their wealth but also their strong Christian beliefs. Having been influenced by D. L. Moody many years before, Henry happily took on the task of reorganizing and reenvisioning the Moody Bible Institute after Moody's death. He funded missionary ventures and church projects on a continual basis. He committed himself to giving to over one hundred charities and Christian causes. In alignment with God's promises, the more he gave, the more he prospered. True to his promise to God when he was a young man, Henry Crowell stayed unknown and anonymous most of his life. "I'll do your work, God, and I'll keep my name out of it," he had said.

Hardly anyone today would recognize his name or know him as an industrial pioneer. He was incredibly influential in sharing his Christian faith and blessing God's kingdom. In October 1943, Henry passed away on his way home on a commuter train. He was reading the Bible. By this time, he had given away 70 percent of his wealth to charitable Christian causes, such as the Crowell Trust and the Moody Bible Institute. He left a legacy of what it means to be a true Christian businessperson.

Chapter 6

THERE'S A SMILE IN EVERY HERSHEY'S BAR

Milton S. Hershey, 1857–1945

What good is money unless you use it to the benefit of the community and of humanity in general?

—Milton Hershey

The hat was a goner. Definitely a goner. Milton looked down into the printing press at the straw hat he had just dropped, now covered in ink and dented. It seemed to be looking mournfully at him. Milton could almost hear it speak, "You're a failure, Milton Hershey. Just like your father before you. Are you ever going to succeed at anything?"

He sighed and reached in to pick up his damaged hat. He'd tried so hard at the apprenticeship that his father had found for him when he'd dropped out of school after fourth grade. Mostly, he'd wanted to work so that his family would be stable and not have to keep moving all the time. But now, he'd be fired for his clumsiness. There went his chance to make something of himself and to make his mother proud. Maybe his neighbors were right in what they thought of him: he would end up like his father, always chasing get-rich-quick schemes and failing at every venture he tried.

"Milton!"

Milton turned his head when he heard his boss's voice.

"You're fired. Go home, son. You can't stay here."

Dragging his feet, Milton trudged back to his home in Nine Points, Pennsylvania, where he knew his mother, Fanny, would be waiting. She believed in him, but she had believed in his father too, until he had failed one too many times and left home. What would he do now? He might not know what *he* would do, but he knew what his mom would do. After her morning prayers, she would put him to work doing chores.

"There's nothing like an appreciation for hard work," she constantly told him.

Milton wasn't so sure about that. He had a sneaking suspicion that his appreciation for caramel was stronger than his enjoyment of hard work. When he had money, he would buy himself candies in town and savor them throughout the day. His favorite candy was caramel. He loved the way it stuck to his teeth. Next to that was his appreciation of Swiss chocolate.

As he kicked his feet along the road, the thought came to him: *I could make caramels.* His imagination sparked as he saw himself in a candy store, selling sweets to young people just like him. He wasn't interested in being a printer. He never had been interested in that. But he loved candy. He loved the idea of inventing new sweets and trying new recipes. This might be an idea where he could finally succeed. Anyway, he could at least try—right?

Fanny Hershey, whose belief in her only son was absolute, found Milton a position with a master confectioner in Lancaster. This time, he didn't get fired from his apprenticeship, and four years later, he was qualified to make candy. Milton's imagination fired up when he thought about owning his own candy store. Much of the nation was beginning to move to larger cities. Nearby Philadelphia was no exception. He knew this city's growth would create sweet moneymaking opportunities.

"Aunt Mattie, I wonder if you would loan me some money," he said to his aunt one day. "I'd like to start my own candy store in Philadelphia."

At nineteen years old and with $150 in his pocket, he headed to Philadelphia and set up a store on his own. Initially, the new store was profitable, as crowds were drawn to visit. Unfortunately, this new interest did not last long enough. No matter how hard he worked, he couldn't sell enough candy to stay afloat. Eventually, Milton didn't have enough money to pay his bills, and he was forced to file for bankruptcy.

In his eyes, it was a monumental failure. He didn't allow this to discourage him from following his dream, though. His vision of being a successful candymaker was still alive. Four years later, he decided to give the candy store idea another try. *Surely it was just the struggling economy,* he thought.

This time, his optimism gave him new vision and direction for success. Although he had high hopes, this new storefront was also unsuccessful. He went bankrupt again. This was the second time he had filed bankruptcy, and he was only twenty-six years old.

If he was going to end up like his father, he might as well go out and visit him, Milton thought. He traveled to Denver to spend time with him. He'd heard his father was looking for silver in the mines and thought he could do the same. Unfortunately, when he arrived, he found there was no silver. His father was once again out of work.

Milton decided to seek employment with a local caramel candy company instead. This was employment he knew he could enjoy. Milton didn't know it when he started, but that job would give him the secret ingredient he needed to move from failure to success.

"You're using milk?" Milton asked his boss as he watched him make candy one day. "For the caramels?"

"Sure. It makes them creamy." His boss took a jar of caramels off a shelf and passed it to Milton. "Try one."

Milton bit into the soft, delicious caramel and was immediately transfixed. The creaminess of the milk gave the sticky caramel a smooth chewiness and a delightful flavor.

"That's delicious," he said. "Show me how?"

Using fresh milk in his caramels was what Milton had been missing. It was the secret ingredient that would make him rich, but he had no money to invest in the idea. When he headed back to Pennsylvania in 1886, he imagined his relatives whispering about him as he passed by.

"Irresponsible drifter."

"He wasted all that money from his aunt."

"Twice bankrupted."

But Milton had three people still in his corner. One was his mother. The second was his friend William Lebkicher, who had worked for him in Philadelphia. His third encourager was his aunt Mattie, whose purse strings were still open for a loan. They had no doubt that he would eventually triumph with his sweet ideas.

Milton began to develop what would become his renowned Hershey's Crystal, a caramel candy. He made it during the day and took it out in the evening, selling to passersby from a handcart.

"It melts in your mouth," said William, after trying it. "This is the one. Should we advertise?"

"Give them quality," said Milton. "That's the best kind of advertising."

Milton was a strong believer in word-of-mouth advertising. The quality of his caramel did speak for itself, and word spread quickly. His business grew rapidly, but he was not just in the business to make money. He generously shared his proceeds with others, his donations rising as his income rose.

"Milton, look at this," his mother said one day, holding up a letter. "It's a large order from England for the caramels."

"Show me," said Milton. He read the letter and gasped. "That's the largest candy order I've ever received. We are going to sell internationally. God is blessing our business!"

It was the beginning of significant success for Milton Hershey. His business, the Lancaster Caramel Company, grew and began to make substantial profits.

Milton enjoyed traveling to visit candy factories and exhibitions. He visited them internationally and throughout America. At an exhibition in Chicago, he came across innovative German chocolate-making equipment. It sparked his imagination.

Caramels are only a fad, he thought. *Chocolate is a permanent thing.*

He set up the Hershey Chocolate Company in 1894 when he was thirty-seven years of age. He taught himself how to make chocolate. By 1900, he was ready to sell the Lancaster Caramel Company for a million dollars and focus entirely on mass-producing milk chocolate bars.

"I believed that if I put a chocolate on the market that was better than anyone else was making, or was likely to make, and keep it absolutely uniform in quality," he said, "the time would come when the public would appreciate it and buy it" (Prabook n.d.).

The public did appreciate his chocolate bars, and they bought them by the masses. Milton quickly realized he would need larger facilities if he wanted to keep up with demand. Together with his wife, Catherine, whom he had married in 1898, Milton returned to his birthplace of Derry County, Pennsylvania, to build what would become the largest chocolate factory in the world. He was seeking a place with cows for fresh milk, a dedicated workforce, and a good source of water. Derry County provided all of these.

But Milton was not just interested in building a factory. He wanted to build a model town as well. Manufacturing towns that had sprung up at the time were not comfortable or beautiful places to live. Those towns didn't give the workers a good quality of life. Milton wanted to provide something entirely different for his employees. The town he built would become known as Hershey, Pennsylvania. His mother had always inspired him with biblical teachings, and Milton followed the Golden Rule—"Do unto others as you would have them do unto you." For Milton, looking after his employees was *doing unto others*.

"If you're doing well, you have to look after others," he told himself. "It's a responsibility."

To begin with, he built a post office and boarding house for factory employees. As the town grew, he also opened a public park and planted gardens for the residents. He then built a bank to provide a way for employees to own and build their own homes in the town. Afterward, he built churches, schools, and recreational facilities to ensure his employees lived comfortable lives in Hershey, Pennsylvania.

Milton's business shrewdness kept the Hershey company growing throughout the Great Depression and both World Wars. His company became the leading name in chocolate and cocoa. His creativity came into play once again when he developed and named the famous Hershey's Kiss in 1907. This proved to be one of the most innovative chocolates the world has ever known.

In his personal life, however, things were not so pleasant. Milton and his wife had dreamed of starting a family but were unable to have children. The Hersheys birthed a different desire. They used the bulk of their savings to set up the Hershey Industrial School, which looked after orphan boys. This school was eventually renamed Milton Hershey School. It now serves more than 1,900 children and is a wonderful place for children to receive an education.

Milton said, "One is only happy in proportion to how he makes others feel happy" (Shell and Kraft 2014).

Another time, when he was asked to give advice, Milton said, "Be honest; train yourself for useful work; love God" (Prabook n.d.).

The greatest love of Milton's life was his wife, Catherine. Tragically, Catherine died young due to a debilitating disease of the nervous system. In March 1915, after Milton was called to her side, they lovingly said their last goodbyes. Catherine passed away at only forty-three years old. It was the end of a very happy marriage. Milton never remarried, and he carried a picture of Catherine with him for the remainder of his life.

In overcoming grief, Milton spent much of his time working. Following his mother's teaching about hard work, Milton continued to work well into his eighties. Those who worked with him spoke of his perseverance and his constant concern for others. He lived long enough to see the end of World War II, passing away in a hospital in 1945.

The Hershey Chocolate Company is still one of the world's finest candy-making companies, and Milton's example of quality and generosity, along with his belief in the golden rule and his work with the orphanage, remain a strong part of his legacy. If Milton Hershey had given up when he faced failure and not followed the spark of his vibrant imagination, the world today would be a lot less sweet.

Chapter 7

A LITTLE TASTE OF HEAVEN

James L. Kraft, 1874–1953

The only investment I ever made which has paid consistently increasing dividends is the money I have given to the Lord.

—James L. Kraft

He looked quite weird, talking to his horse in the middle of the street, but James did not really care how things looked that day. He'd had it. His feet were sore from walking from store to store, and even though he was working extremely hard, he just didn't seem to be getting ahead.

"Paddy, I need a business partner," he said to his horse. He waited for a moment, but Paddy did nothing. James smiled to himself. What did he expect Paddy to do? Open his mouth and start speaking? Growing up on a dairy farm in Canada, he'd been around enough animals to know they were great at listening but not so good at giving advice.

Of course, his mother was excellent at telling him what to do. In his head, James could hear her most common piece of advice.

"Pray about it," she had said repeatedly. "If you have a problem, bring it to the Lord. He'll always help you."

He'd always prayed, of course. There was no escaping prayer in their conservative Mennonite household. Bedtime prayers took a while as all eleven children had their turns.

Now, James really needed help. He had been pushed out of a company he'd invested in, and he only had sixty-five dollars left. Then, his mother's second-most-common piece of advice had played in his head.

"Work hard, son. Keep on going. Never quit."

He had to keep trying. James was used to hard work. On the farm, there had always been more to do. He wasn't one to curl up in the corner and lick his wounds, no matter how difficult it was. His business was wrapped around his favorite food—cheese. He knew he was destined to create the greatest cheese company in the world. So far, though, it hadn't been profitable.

"Paddy, what am I going to do?" he asked.

Paddy had been the answer to his first problem. James had noticed that storeowners were going to a wholesale warehouse to buy cheese. If he could make it more convenient for them to get their cheese, perhaps they would buy from him instead. He rented Paddy and a cart, then began delivering cheese directly to the stores. At the time, it was unheard of to deliver goods directly to the grocery store owners.

The grocery stores were happy with him, but his business still wasn't very profitable. The days were long, and the constant traveling was difficult. The other problem James had was that the cheese quickly spoiled. If their cheese went bad, the grocery stores had to throw it out. No shop owner wanted to risk buying too much cheese from James, no matter how good it was. If they couldn't sell it quickly enough, it would mean they would have a loss.

"I'm doing my best," he told Paddy, "but it just isn't working out."

In his head, James heard his mother's voice again. It was another piece of advice she had constantly given her children: "Give your best to God."

James had an epiphany.

"That's it, Paddy! That's what we need to do. I need to pray and put God first." He thumped his fist on his knee and turned toward his horse. "Paddy, I'm going to give 25 percent of my profits to God."

It was the turning point for James's business. His business supernaturally became more profitable when he put God first. He became known for supplying the highest-quality cheese throughout Chicago. His business grew, and in 1909, he brought four of his brothers in to work with him. Something, however, still troubled him.

The cheese was spoiling. If only he could figure out a way to create a cheese that lasted longer on the shelf and consistently tasted good—that was his greatest challenge.

Lying in bed one night, he thought back to his days on the dairy farm. "We pasteurized the milk," he said to himself, "which made it last longer. If I could somehow bring that idea into cheesemaking ..."

Inspired, James thought about ways to make cheese that would last, as he made his daily deliveries. If he could somehow blend it with pasteurized milk and package it in sterile containers, it wouldn't spoil so quickly.

For months, James worked by day and experimented by night. He failed time after time but refused to quit.

In 1915, after years of trying, he finally found the answer for which he had been praying. With the right amount of heat and a certain type of processing, James could make a cheese that was everything he had hoped. This epiphany would change the world of cheese making.

James's breakthrough came at just the right time. World War I was underway, and soldiers needed to eat nutritious food that could be shipped out to them without spoiling. James's canned cheese was the perfect ration. The American government bought millions of dollars' worth of cheese, and his company exploded in size overnight.

Growing his business, James started to send his products overseas. In America, people were eating 50 percent more cheese than they had before, largely because of his products. In 1928, his company employed ten thousand people and sold about one-third of all the cheese sold domestically (Sponholtz 2000).

James's mother's advice had stayed with him. He always brought his problems to God in prayer, trusting that he would receive an answer. He assumed whatever answer remained in his mind was an answer from God, and this proved correct.

James continued to take the idea of giving to God very seriously. He gave at least 25 percent of his personal profits to God from the day he had that conversation with Paddy. Some sources indicate that by the end of his life, he was giving *all* his personal profits to God. He certainly wasn't content to give only 10 percent. He often said that tithing was a good place to start but that one should give much more than what was required.

James's generosity wasn't shown just through the giving of his own money. In 2015, there was a merger between H. J. Heinz Company and Kraft Foods Group. Both companies shared similar philosophies on charitable giving. As of 2020, Heinz-Kraft Foods is still going strong with more than thirty-eight thousand employees operating in over two hundred countries. Kraft Foods has also made large donations of food and humanitarian efforts continually. Today, Kraft continues to work with nonprofit organizations, like Feeding America and Save the Children in Southeast Asia (Mullen and Galia 2020).

From an investment of sixty-seven dollars in a horse and cart in 1903, James Kraft's business grew to be worth over $136 billion in 2018. James became a wealthy and successful man but consistently said that God came first. He taught Sunday school as a member of the North Shore Baptist Church. "I would rather be a layman in the North Shore Baptist Church than head up the largest corporation in America," he said. "My first job is to serve Jesus" (Joy Christian Ministries 2015).

Over his life, James received several honorary doctorates and the Gutenberg Award of the Chicago Bible Society in 1952. Sadly, in 1953, at the age of seventy-eight, James Kraft died from surgical complications.

His legacy, however, remained strong. His habits of hard work, prayer, and putting God first built a company that became one of the most recognizable in the world.

Today, as millions of people eat Kraft products, they might think about James Kraft back in 1903 and the conversation he had with his horse that transformed his company.

Chapter 8

EVERY DAY MATTERS

James Cash Penney, 1875–1971

The Golden Rule finds no limit of application in business.

—James Cash Penney

Tears streamed freely down eight-year-old Jimmy's cheeks. He knelt alongside his bed, trying not to think about the throbbing, painful blisters on his feet. The cardboard he had been using since the real soles had worn out had not worked that day. The rain had ruined the cardboard, and the sharp rocks in the farm soil had damaged his feet. Although the pain was immense, it was not the reason he was crying. He wept because he couldn't think of a solution.

"Lord, you are my Provider. I put my trust in you," he cried out. "I need your help."

Jimmy didn't know it, but the answer to his simple bedtime prayer, as a young boy with sore feet, paved the way for him to grow up to become a person of integrity.

From an early age, Jimmy had helped his father run their farm. He enjoyed the early morning routine—waking up before sunrise and heading straight out to the barn to milk his favorite cow, Blossom. Jimmy's father, James, was a hard worker and kept a close watch on his livestock and fields, walking around the farm each morning to ensure that all the animals were being cared for and fed. He also pastored a local church, where Jimmy's grandfather was a minister as well. James was committed to raising his son to become a man of integrity. In fact, both Jimmy's pa and grandpa teamed up on many occasions to sow seeds of integrity from God's Word into Jimmy's heart.

The morning after Jimmy's prayer for shoes, James walked into the barn to check up on his son who was humming his favorite church hymn and rhythmically pulling on the patient cow.

"This little light of mine." Tug. "I'm going to let it shine." Tug again.

"Where are your shoes, boy?" James asked.

Jimmy was not supposed to be in the barn barefooted. It was too dangerous with the cows. His feet could be stepped on and crushed, or Jimmy might step in something dirty or get sick. It was cold without shoes. "My shoes are in my room, Pa," said Jimmy, turning his head to look at his father.

"Are you trying to catch a cold, son? Is that what you're trying to do?"

"Pa, let me explain." Jimmy knew he was in trouble. He told his father about the rain. "I need some new shoes, Pa. Will you buy me some?"

His father was quiet for a moment. All Jimmy could hear was the low *chew, chew, chew* as Blossom munched on her feed.

"I don't want you to get sick, son," said James, eventually. "You know we can't afford for you to see a doctor. Finish up with Blossom, and then get on inside. Wait for me in my study room."

This was bad news. If they were going to meet in the study room, Jimmy was in deeper trouble than he expected, but he couldn't figure it out. How could he be punished for not wearing shoes if he didn't *have* any shoes?

By the time James walked into the study, Jimmy was one nervous eight-year-old. His father sat down and looked sternly at his son for a moment.

"Don't think I've brought you in here because you're in trouble. You're not. I brought you to my study room because you are old enough for us to have a real conversation—man to man."

Jimmy asked quickly, "Do we have money to buy me shoes?"

The direct question seemed to catch James off guard. Jimmy had never seen his hardworking, responsible father look so shaken. He knew—they all knew—that these were difficult times. The whispered conversations between his parents over the supper table and the head shaking when two farmers got together to talk was just a small indication of the problem at hand. Tears formed in James's eyes as he began to speak.

"I have something very important that I must explain to you. It has been difficult for me and your mom to provide for you children lately. We don't have money to buy you new shoes. As a matter of fact, we don't have money to buy you any clothes at all. We can barely feed ourselves at this point." His dad took a deep breath. "If you want some shoes bad enough, you are just going to have to find a way to buy yourself some."

Jimmy looked at his father, shocked, but then he was suddenly filled with enthusiasm. His pa believed in him! James, his father who was always in charge, had given Jimmy permission to do something about his situation. That kind of encouragement must mean there was *something* Jimmy could do to earn the money he needed.

An idea came to him. *Why, the melons have just ripened. We grow the best melons in this entire county. And the county fair is this weekend, just two miles down the road.*

Jimmy woke before sunrise that Saturday morning and quickly loaded the wagon full of delicious, perfectly ripe melons that he and his father had harvested just a day or so before. Full of confident anticipation, the young boy set off toward the fairground. His wares were perfect. He would sell lots of melons and have enough money in his hand to buy a good, sturdy pair of shoes. He could almost imagine them on his feet.

But when he arrived at the gate of the county fair, he was confronted with an unexpected obstacle.

"Pay your fee, sonny," said the man at the entrance, as Jimmy tried to go in through the gate. "All vendors pay the fee."

"I'm just selling melons," Jimmy protested, but the man shook his head and pursed his lips.

"All vendors," he emphasized.

Jimmy turned out his pockets. He didn't have money to pay the gatekeeper to get into the county fair. There was no way he could go in to make money selling his melons. There was no way he could buy his shoes. Or was there?

Jimmy parked his wagon full of melons a little way from the entrance to the fairgrounds and called out to people as they approached the gate.

Much to his delight, customers soon flocked to his wagon and purchased melons by the dozen. After a while, Jimmy realized that he needed to sell just a few more melons to have enough money to get some brand-new shoes. He felt like a warrior on the verge of winning his first battle.

In the midst of Jimmy's selling frenzy, a man suddenly jumped from an approaching wagon and grabbed him by the shoulders.

"What do you think you're doing?" he yelled.

Startled, Jimmy turned to face his dismayed father. "I'm just trying to sell enough melons to buy me some shoes, Pa," Jimmy answered in a small, frightened voice.

"Listen to me, son—what you are doing is wrong. The people in that fair paid full price to sell their produce. You're taking advantage of them. You didn't pay anything to compete against them. How would you like it if they used illegal tactics to compete against you?" As his father knelt on the ground, Jimmy was forced to look into his father's serious eyes. "Remember this commandment, and don't you ever forget it: You ought to 'do to others as you would have them do to you'" (Luke 6:31 NIV).

The sounds of the fair were muted in the background as Jimmy's father kept talking.

"Listen to me closely. It is not by coincidence that the shoes you are wearing have holes in the bottom. Your feet wouldn't be full of blisters right now if the owner of the local clothing store was a man of integrity. He sold us defective shoes. God is teaching you something. You must have integrity in all your business dealings, and He will help you succeed."

James's words penetrated deep into Jimmy's eight-year-old heart on that busy, dusty road. The seeds that were sown that day would reap a great harvest. With his father's help and guidance, Jimmy paid the fee and moved his wagon into the county fair. He sold all his melons and earned the money he needed to purchase new shoes. Shopping carefully, he purchased the best-looking, highest-quality pair that he could afford.

"Nice shoes, Jimmy," said his friends when they saw him at school the next day. "They look sharp."

Jimmy felt proud and pleased. He had learned a principle that would stick with him all his life: a clothing store should keep its integrity while selling nice, well-made, and high-quality products at affordable prices.

As an adult, Jimmy came to be called "Golden Rule Penney." He continued to uphold the standard of integrity he learned from his father and grandfather—the standard given by Jesus Christ. He began a retail clothing store franchise, originally known as the Golden Rule Stores. You might recognize Jimmy by the name of James *Cash* Penney. His stores were later renamed JCPenney, but Jimmy remained unwilling to sell cheap clothes, like those defective shoes he had worn as a child. He sold only things that were well-made and of good quality.

The success of the JCPenney stores saw Jimmy become the largest retailer in the United States. His integrity led to his achievements, and his achievements opened doors for him. Golden Rule Penny learned a lesson about integrity from his father that changed the course of his life and provided millions of people with good-quality products that wouldn't fail.

> So, in everything, do to others what you would have them
> do to you, for this sums up the Law and the Prophets.
> —Matthew 7:12 (NIV)

Chapter 9

PURE SQUEEZED SUNSHINE

Anthony T. Rossi, 1900–1993

God loves me. And all God does is for my own good.
—Anthony Rossi

The first glimmer of light was beginning to show in the cool, quiet December morning. There was a hush across the beautiful Italian city in Sicily. Only enthusiastic early risers, like eight-year-old Anthony, were up and ready for breakfast at this hour.

Anthony Rossi grinned to himself. Soon, he'd have some delicious breakfast. He rubbed his tummy in anticipation. Brioche and fresh orange juice—mmm. After that, he'd make his brothers go outside and play. It would be a good day for mischief and fun. He looked at the clock. It was only 5:15. His mother wouldn't be up for a while, and even then, the fire wouldn't be started, or the bread brought out of the pantry. He'd have to wait. He waited and waited.

He waited as long as any eight-year-old boy could be expected to wait. He looked at the clock again—5:17. He sighed. *Oh well.* Perhaps he could think of a new way to annoy the priest at mass. Perhaps something funny and easy to blame on his sister.

Out of nowhere came a thundering noise and a sudden shaking. Anthony put out his hand to steady himself, but the house itself was rocking. Outside, it sounded like torrential rain was dumped on the roof. He opened his mouth to cry out, but the noise changed again. This time it sounded like a terrible, terrifying whistling sound. The house quit shaking, and the walls shifted violently.

"Help!" The screams of Anthony's family filled the rooms. Children came running, terrified and whimpering. What was happening? No one seemed to know.

Anthony and his family had survived the extraordinary earthquake of Messina, Sicily, in 1908. His family narrowly escaped destruction. Around eighty thousand people lost their lives that morning. Most of the dead had been sound asleep when the shaking started and never sensed the approaching calamity.

Anthony sobbed. "What does it mean?" he asked his father. "What is God doing? Is it judgment?"

There were few answers and plenty of work to do to clean up the damage and rebuild the town. A year of aftershocks reminded Anthony of his questions about God. He would be on a quest to find those answers for decades to come.

***

From the deck of the ship, Anthony gasped in excitement at the sight of the Statue of Liberty. In 1921, the voyage to America from Sicily took weeks, but twenty-one-year-old Rossi didn't mind. He was young, enthusiastic, and full of plans.

"We'll get jobs and make enough money to go to Africa and make a film," he said to his three friends before they even boarded the ship. In was in Anthony's personality to have big dreams and constantly form new plans. When they arrived, Anthony only had thirty dollars in his pocket, and he didn't speak any English.

"*Buongiorno*," he said, nodding to everyone he met. No one replied, and he realized he had some work to do. Anthony quickly forgot his filmmaking dreams as he worked hard to earn his keep. He took jobs as a taxi driver, mechanic's helper, and waiter. He then saved up enough money to purchase a grocery store on Long Island that he continued to operate for thirteen years.

Business was good, but the New York weather didn't suit him. He craved the Sicilian sunshine and warmth that he had so loved as a child. He didn't want to go back to Italy, but he knew there must be another alternative. Perhaps he could relocate somewhere else.

In his early forties, Anthony Rossi's life had two big upheavals. The first was moving to Florida. The warmth of the climate was more like his childhood home of Sicily—and they grew oranges there! His favorite breakfast juice would be on the menu once again. Rossi initially got a job on a farm, growing tomatoes. He saved money once again and eventually launched a new venture. This time, it was a restaurant.

The second upheaval was a spiritual one. Rossi developed a great desire to read the Bible. All those questions about God and judgment that arose from the earthquake when he was eight began to be answered. He realized God's Word gave an answer for all life's most difficult questions. The Bible said God was slow to anger and abounding in love.

God is merciful, Anthony realized. *Abounding in love. He is not quick to judge.*

God's Word said that life would have problems and tribulations, but it also said that God would provide His Holy Spirit to give comfort after such trials. Anthony realized his family had not experienced judgment when he was eight years old. Instead, they had experienced deliverance and protection. Reading the Bible gave Anthony a new devotion that entirely transformed his life.

In Florida, Anthony and his wife, Sana, joined the First Methodist Church. When they eventually settled in Brenton, Florida, they became members of Calvary Baptist Church. Pleasing God became most important in the Rossi household. In his faith, he found peace for all the difficult questions he had as a child. His faith gave him the strength and resolve to endure the tribulations of life. If he had a problem, he prayed about it and, in Christ, found peace.

Although the restaurant business didn't work out, Rossi had a new business idea. Florida was famous for its citrus fruit, including oranges, and Anthony knew several businesspeople in New York. He decided to sell gift boxes of Florida oranges to businesses in New York City. This venture was successful, and Rossi's business expanded. He began selling not only whole citrus fruit but also squeezed orange juice.

In the 1950s, he invented a new way to pack and ship juice. With his new method, orange juice could be stored without refrigeration and would last for three months on a shelf. This was revolutionary and opened more opportunities for his company, Tropicana Orange Juice.

Anthony was known as the Father of Chilled Juice in Florida (Florida Citrus Hall of Fame n.d.), and he worked hard until he retired in 1978. He sold his business for a massive $500 million.

He used a portion of his finances to support Christian missions, such as starting Bradenton Missionary Village, a retirement community in Florida for missionaries. He also began an organization called Bible Alliance that created and mailed audio tapes of scripture in dozens of languages to the mission field. Over three hundred thousand blind people were able to receive audio Bibles from this ministry of sending "little missionaries" all over the world (Aurora Ministries n.d.). In 1983, *Town and Country* magazine named Anthony Rossi one of the top ten most generous living Americans.

Anthony gave God all the glory for his success. He was known to be a man of prayer. When he needed a new idea or the solution to a problem, he sought God for help. In turn, God developed Anthony into a great business leader who used his business sense to help others. He died in 1993, at the age of ninety-two. God's supernatural blessing was always present in his life. God knew Anthony had a great purpose—to use his business gift to be a blessing to the world—and Anthony fulfilled his purpose by giving generously from what he made.

Chapter 10

SAVE MONEY—LIVE BETTER

Samuel Walton, 1918–1992

Common looking people are the best in the world: that is
the reason the Lord makes so many of them.

—Abraham Lincoln

"Stop it, Sammy," yelled Sam's younger brother, Bob. He shook the warm
milk off his shirt. "You've squirted me again. It's disgusting."

"Ha-ha, it's funny!" Sam said with a laugh, but he went over to his
brother. "I'm sorry."

"You did it on purpose." Bob was still angry.

Sam had to agree. Squirting Bob with the milk from the cow's udders
made the dark, cold mornings in the milking shed more fun, but he
felt bad.

"I'll finish your part of the milking if you like," he offered as a peace-
making gesture.

"Fine. I'll swap you for the chickens," Bob said.

Both boys had helped around the family farm from an early age. On
a farm, everyone had to pitch in, and Sam didn't mind that. But he still
had a desire to make his own money and do something for himself. It was
an idea that grew and grew in his mind, until one morning, at the age
of eight, he woke up exceedingly early with his heart hammering with

excitement. His plan was complete. Somehow, he knew exactly what he was going to do. Full of excitement, he ran down the still-dark hall to his parents' bedroom and banged on their door.

"Daddy, answer the door!"

Startled, Sam's dad, William, bolted from his bed and quickly opened the door. "What's wrong, Sam?"

Sam was jumping up and down with enthusiasm. "I have an idea."

William settled into a comfortable chair and rubbed the sleep from his eyes. He pulled his oldest son over and stood the boy squarely in front of him. "Well, Sam, what is it? Tell me what's on your mind."

Taking a deep and serious breath, Sam looked his dad straight in the eyes, his gaze steady. "I think it's about time we had a serious conversation about all the hard work I've been doing around this farm."

Sam's dad chuckled. "Oh?"

Sam continued, "In fact, I think it's about time I go into business for myself."

Sitting in the cool, still dawn, watching his earnest barefoot child, William's first impulse was to laugh, but as he considered Sam's stern look, he recognized that his son had inherited his own entrepreneurial determination.

William clasped Sam's hand in a firm shake. "Son, if you think it's time to go into business for yourself, you go for it. You are a humble boy with great courage, and if you set your mind to it, you can do anything."

William was himself a businessman, but not everyone admired the business in which he engaged—repossessing properties for a mortgage company that was owned by his brother.

His father's permission was all the motivation Sam needed, and he immediately began preparations for his first venture. The fields and woods surrounding the farm teemed with wildlife. Sam set traps all around the area, and he soon caught and prepared a substantial inventory of pigeons and rabbits.

Sam's Pigeon and Rabbit Stand performed better than the average stands in Sam's neighborhood. He developed his natural gift for business and was soon doing quite well.

William had diligently taught Sam to be modest and humble in all his actions. Even though his business allowed the family to live comfortably, nobody really knew that Sam's family was better off than most. His family dressed and lived just like all the other struggling farm families in Missouri. Young Sam had learned well and remained a humble eight-year-old entrepreneur, never bragging or boasting. This early philosophy of humility made a deep impression on Sam's life and would stay with him in his prosperity.

While walking home one afternoon, fourteen-year-old Sam heard the voice of a boy crying out from a nearby river.

"Help! I'm drowning!"

Sam didn't think about his own safety. He dived into the water and pulled the boy out. By that time, the boy was unconscious and not breathing, but Sam performed CPR until the boy began to breathe on his own.

"You saved my life!" the boy gasped.

"Don't even mention it," Sam responded with his trademark modesty.

The community considered Sam a hero, and the rescue made the local headlines. Sam felt embarrassed when asked to talk about the incident as an adult. He never wanted to appear as though he was bragging or as though he was an important hero.

Sam met his future wife, Helen, at the University of Missouri, where they were both earning degrees in business. After they married, they decided to start a business together, so in 1945, when Sam was twenty-seven, they moved to Newport, Arkansas, where they purchased a Ben Franklin retail store for $25,000. The store was not performing well when they purchased it, but within two years, Sam had turned it into the most profitable Ben Franklin retail outlet in a six-state region.

Sam and Helen Walton eventually moved to Bentonville, Arkansas, and with the help of Sam's brother, Bob, they began a larger retail franchise. The first store, Wal-Mart Discount City, opened in 1962. The business performed well, and Sam became extremely wealthy.

What made his business unique was the idea of "service leadership," which was based on the fundamental stated by Jesus in Matthew 20:28: "Just as the Son of Man did not come to be served, but to serve, and to give his life as a ransom for many."

Those who wanted to earn promotions within the company were evaluated in their level of servanthood and how they interacted with others.

In 1991, with very little known about him, Sam Walton was named the richest man in America. Reporters flocked to his hometown in Bentonville to get a better idea of who he was. But as they investigated his story, they were amazed by Sam Walton's lifestyle. The richest man in America blended in just like a common guy, driving an old beat-up pickup truck with hunting dogs in the back and wearing a baseball cap, jeans, and a T-shirt to work. People were taken aback by his humble ways. This was not the typical lifestyle of a billionaire.

"What do they expect me to do?" asked Sam in bewilderment. "Take my dogs around in a Rolls-Royce?"

Sam realized he had been bestowed a gift from God to make money and that he was to use it to help others. The Wal-Mart associates were amazed by Sam's evangelical ways. Their boss was passionate about the success of Wal-Mart but not for himself. His vision was to improve the quality of life for people by lowering their cost of living.

"Mr. Walton has a calling," said the vice president of Wal-Mart.

Others said that he spoke like a fiery Baptist preacher.

Ever the ordinary guy, Sam didn't carry around much money. On business trips, Sam often ran out of cash and asked a colleague, Daniel Gould, to loan him some.

"Does Sam have money?" Gould would say. "I've been traveling with him for thirty years, and you could never tell it. In fact, I'd say he was broke."

True to his father's teaching, even as a man with a net worth of $28 billion dollars, Sam didn't feel any need to carry around a fat wallet or drive around in flashy cars.

Sam Walton simply rejected pride and embraced humility. He flew first class only one time in his life.

Bernard Marcus, cofounder of Home Depot, once drove with Sam in his pickup truck. Later, he commented on the lack of air conditioning and the coffee stains on the seats. He referred to Sam Walton as a humble man.

Humility was one of Sam's competitive advantages in growing Wal-Mart. While competitors often withdrew capital from a young company to live a prestigious lifestyle, he had no need for such a vain goal. Sam Walton was content to stay out of the public eye as much as possible. If he could sneak away on Sunday to go quail hunting after church, that satisfied him plenty.

In 1987, Sam Walton began the Walton Family Foundation. This foundation, which has been continually supported by Walton's descendants, supports three areas: K–12 education, protecting clean water sources, and investing in Arkansas, Walton's home region. Between 2014 and 2018, this foundation gave more than $2.3 billion specifically toward education. While Walton was not the type of Christian to preach on street corners, he had a passionate burden to serve others. This burden is carried on by his children and children's children.

> God resists the proud, But gives grace to the humble.
> —James 4:6 (NKJV)

Chapter 11

IF YOU THINK YOU CAN, YOU CAN

Mary Kay Ash, 1918–2001

A girl nowadays must believe completely in herself as an individual. She must realize at the outset that a woman must do the same job better than a man to get as much credit for it. She must be aware of the various discriminations, both legal and traditional, against women in the business world.

—Amelia Earhart (1935)

It was her first board meeting in her role as a manager in the company. Mary was both nervous and brimming with excitement to enter the elegant but intimidating boardroom with its polished wood surfaces. Her hard work and success in direct sales had won her this exciting position. A woman in management was a rare thing for the early 1960s, and Mary was the only woman to hold such a position at World Gift. After years of hard work, she would finally be able to demonstrate to Sam, the company's president, that she also had good leadership ideas.

The room filled with the other managers—all men, of course—nodding to each other, greeting each other, and making jokes. Mary controlled her anxious emotions as the meeting got underway. She felt as if she carried the responsibility to speak for all the women in the company, and she had long anticipated this opportunity to present her management ideas to the board members.

With a passion to share a message dear to her heart, Mary wanted to help women be self-confident and have high self-esteem. This message was so important to Mary that she believed God had commissioned her to share it with women worldwide.

"So, Mary," said Sam. "What ideas do you have on how to help our saleswomen be more effective?"

Mary gathered her courage. "I'm glad you asked," she began confidently, sitting up straight and smiling. "I think our organization needs to be more responsive to the emotional needs of our saleswomen. We should have employee meetings where we invite motivational speakers who will encourage our sales reps to have better self-esteem. They will not only become more confident salespeople, but we will also be improving their overall quality of life."

To Mary's surprise, the entire management staff started laughing. Their deep guffaws echoed through the room.

"You're thinking like a woman again, Mary," Sam said, still chuckling.

Mary narrowed her eyes. "And how's that?"

"You're just so sensitive." He sat back and crossed his arms. "Why would we focus on the self-esteem of our employees? We care about improving profit margins. I have a better idea. One that'll *motivate* them."

Here he goes again, Mary thought, *with his misogynistic statements.*

"I think we should cut the size of our workforce."

Her colleagues sat up with nods of approval of Sam's statement.

"When employees feel their job security is at risk, they work harder to keep their jobs. Only employees who are meeting their sales goals will keep their jobs. Everyone who does not meet monthly quotas will be laid off."

Mary stood up abruptly. The other men in the room turned to fix their amused gazes on her. Would she dare confront Sam? She paused for a moment, unwilling to speak, as everyone stared at her. She was tired of management always belittling women as if they were inferior, but if she spoke up for the women in the company, it would ruin her own twenty-five-year career at World Gift. It would be a large sacrifice to make, but if she didn't speak up for the women, who would?

"Do you have a problem with my idea, Mary?" challenged Sam.

"Yes," Mary said firmly. "Yes, I do, Sam. But more importantly, I have a problem with you. These women work their tails off to benefit this organization. How could you be so inconsiderate? They all need their jobs. How dare you talk about firing some of them and take it so lightly? Although some sales are low, I know sales will bounce back to normal as the recent economic decline recovers."

"Mary, stop thinking like a woman!" Sam looked around the room, and the other men nodded in agreement. "This is why women aren't meant to be in administrative positions. Can't you see that, Mary? Sorry, but this capability is just not within your grasp. You make emotional decisions without prioritizing the company's finances."

Now Mary was boiling inside. She pushed her chair back. When he heard the scrape on the floor, Sam sat up straight, paying attention.

"Let me tell you what I'm going to do, Sam. I'm going to walk out this door and start my own business. You are going to see that women can lead. As a matter of fact, you are going to see that I am a better leader than you ever dreamed of becoming. You are going to regret that this company lost me. From this day forward, I am your greatest competitor." She gathered her notes and backed away from the table. "We'll see if a dozen male executives are able to outwit one female entrepreneur," she said. "I quit!"

Poised as ever, Mary held her head high and walked gracefully out of the board meeting. As she passed through the heavy doors, she heard the management team burst out laughing behind her.

"Our Mary sees herself as some sort of an entrepreneur. Can you imagine that?" one of the teasing voices said.

Mary's determination was fueled by their mocking. She had a dream—to start a global business that would treat women equally and give them an equal opportunity of promotion in the workplace. It was a dream that was deeply embedded within her heart, and Mary believed that God would help her attain success. She believed the Bible told her that God was interested in her success.

But how would she get started on this venture? Perhaps the first step was to see an attorney to become a limited liability company. Mary headed off that very day to visit an attorney friend, Cal, to explain what she wanted to do.

"It's a business for women. I want to empower them, encouraging female independence and overall self-esteem. I've got $5,000 in savings to invest, and I'm convinced it will be a huge success," she told him.

Cal grinned while she spoke, as if he was refraining from mocking her idea. "I have a better idea for you," he said.

Mary felt confused.

"Why don't you get your savings and hide it somewhere in your house?" Carl suggested. "Keep the money safe from these plans and ideas in your mind. Maybe bury it in a sofa. If you did that, you wouldn't run the risk of losing your life savings."

Mary straightened her shoulders, bravely absorbing each word like a blow.

Cal grinned at her. "Do yourself a favor, and give up on this lofty, farfetched idea. Stay home as a housewife. It's more appropriate for a woman of your age. I'm sure your husband would agree with me."

Mary stood up without saying a word and walked out of his office.

That same afternoon, Mary went to visit another friend. She did not want to allow any discouragement to hinder her dream. Her friend was also her accountant. She was feeling slightly belittled from the boardroom and the attorney. Heading to his office, she hoped for some encouragement. Unfortunately, he had a similar mindset regarding women starting businesses.

"Women simply aren't entrepreneurs, Mary," he said. "I don't mean to seem condescending, but that's what statistics show us of female businesswomen. The odds are stacked against you. Do you really believe you will overcome all obstacles and achieve success? Even men struggle in entrepreneurship. And you say it will be international?"

For a moment, Mary wanted to give him a piece of her mind, but she held back. *Actions speak louder than words,* she thought. *He will see he is wrong.*

Now Mary was at a crossroads. The two people she had thought would be more than willing to assist her had disparaged her ideas. It was time to go home to her husband, George. *If George doesn't believe in me, I guess it just wasn't meant to be,* she thought.

Mary prepared George's favorite dish for dinner to help persuade him.

"George, there is something I must talk to you about," she began after George had eaten his fill. "First of all, I quit my job today. I was fed up with Sam. I just think he is chauvinistic, and I refuse to continue working for him."

"It's about time," answered George. "I couldn't wait for you to quit, honey. I always disliked that guy." He sat up straight and grinned, wiping his fingers on his napkin. "I knew this delicious dinner had to serve a purpose. What else is on your mind?"

"George, what I am going to tell you is very important to me." Mary's face lit up with enthusiasm. "There is a desire that has consumed my spirit. It is a dream that dwells in the most intimate aspect of my being. I think that God must have given it to me." She reached out to touch her husband's hand. "Hear me out, and if you disagree, please let me know gently."

"What is it, honey?" asked George, taking Mary's hand in his own. "You know I would never discourage you from something that means this much to you. Tell me what it is. I'm with you."

Encouraged, she continued. "I have a vision. My vision is to start a company. I have a business plan for a direct-sales company that will allow women to excel and develop their abilities to lead without being limited by discrimination. This company will be profitable and designate a considerable amount of income to charities. I am determined to start this company. I don't know what I'll do if my dream doesn't become a reality."

Much to her delight, her husband replied, "Mary, listen to me closely. Not only will I support you in this decision, but I am also 100 percent persuaded that your business will succeed. I'm with you. Do whatever is in your heart."

Mary was overcome with passion. Now, nothing would hold her back.

"I'll handle the administrative aspects," George said. "You just go and sell your products."

"I will, honey," said Mary glowing. "We're going to make a great team."

Mary and George worked to make her ideas a reality. One week before the opening of the new business, Mary prepared a delicious breakfast for George to eat while they went over plans together.

From the corner of her eye, Mary saw George fall out of his chair and onto the floor. He clutched his chest and shook. Mary ran to help him. She checked his pulse and realized his heart had stopped beating.

Trembling, she was barely able to reach for the phone to call for help. She waited in sheer terror until the paramedics arrived, but they gave her dreadful news. George had suffered a cardiac arrest and had already passed away. There was nothing they could do. Mary gasped and broke out in a wail of agony.

"How could this be? The man I love has now passed. How can I go on living without my greatest companion?"

For weeks, all Mary had been thinking about was her new business. Now, she had to bury her husband. But would she bury her dream?

At the funeral, her children asked her a question that almost seemed to be inappropriate, considering the setting. "So, Mom, do you still plan to start your business this week?"

"Yes," she responded. "George supported my dream, and even though it doesn't seem to be a good time, I must see what will come of it. I would rather try and fail than to have never tried at all."

"We're with you, Mom," responded her twenty-year-old son. "I know it means a lot to you. Start your business, and we'll help you however we can."

Mary Kay began her business on September 13, 1963. Her dream now generates over $3 billion annually and is a vivid reality for more than 2.4 million Mary Kay Cosmetics consultants worldwide. It is led primarily by women, and it gives generously to charities on a continual basis.

In 1996, Mary Kay founded the Mary Kay Foundation that serves two purposes. First, it focuses on providing donations to cancer research, specifically cancer that affects women. Second, it focuses on providing funds for domestic violence shelters for women. Since 1996, the foundation has given more than $80 million to organizations that work toward these goals.

God gave Mary a dream, and regardless of all the obstacles with which she was confronted, she wouldn't allow her dream to die. She followed the Golden Rule as her guiding philosophy and focused on prioritizing God in both her own life and her employees' lives.

Mary Kay passed on her wisdom by saying,

> My priorities have always been God first, family second, career third. I have found that when I put my life in this order, everything seems to work out. God was my

first priority early in my career when I was struggling to make ends meet. Through the failures and success I have experienced since then, my faith has remained unchecked. ("Celebrating Mary Kay Ash" n.d.)

Mary Kay used her success not to benefit herself but to benefit women in general, always giving and implementing godly examples to those with whom she worked.

She embraced three virtues that were pivotal to her success—she was very giving, she was self-confident, and she was undeterred by the fact that her male colleagues did not believe in her. Despite all the hardships she faced, she stayed optimistic and was determined to give back to all the women in her organization once she achieved success.

Chapter 12

EAT MOR CHIKIN

S. Truett Cathy, 1921–2014

> Putting people before profits is how we've tried to operate
> from the beginning.
>
> —S. Truett Cathy

"Flip the pancakes, Truett. See those bubbles? That means they're ready," his mom called from the other side of the kitchen.

Truett put down the ear of corn he was shucking, picked up his spatula, and carefully eased each pancake over to finish cooking.

"They look good," he said proudly, going back to the basketful of corn where he was working.

"Good boy," said his mother.

"There are lots of hungry people who want them. When they're done, you can go tell the boarders that breakfast is ready."

Truett wiped his hands and took off his apron before opening the door of their tiny kitchen. He knocked on the bedroom doors in the house, letting the two or three boarders in each room know that breakfast was ready. Serving food to hungry people was something Truett enjoyed doing, even as a young boy.

He initially didn't understand why there were so many new people moving into their house. Squeezing him and his siblings into the back rooms was difficult. His dad had mentioned something called the Great Depression, although it did not sound too great at all. Now, his father's job selling insurance wasn't enough to pay the bills.

"You'll all have to pitch in," he'd told Truett and his siblings. "Help your mom."

They helped, and sometimes it felt like they never stopped helping. Truett learned to shuck corn, shell peas, wash dirty dishes, set the table, and flip numerous eggs and pancakes on the grill.

"It's Sunday, Mom," Truett said, as he came back into the kitchen. "Don't you want to go to church?"

His mother sighed. "I'd love to, but look at all this." She gestured around at the kitchen table, piled with food waiting to be prepared. "It won't cook itself, you know. And those folks pay a dollar a day for two meals." She gave him a sharp look. "But you get washed and ready. Even if I can't go, you can."

Truett gave her a sympathetic glance. His mom worked so hard. He'd love to give her a Sunday off so she could attend church, which she loved to do.

"I'll tune the radio for you before I go to Sunday school," he said, "so you can listen to the message." Sunday was Truett's favorite day of the week. He wished his mom could rest and that they could have a family day.

She smiled a thankful smile at him. "You're a kind boy, Truett. It will take you far in life."

Truett enjoyed serving meals to the boarders, but he wanted to help his family even more. Bringing in some extra money would help, he reasoned. At eight years of age, Truett took twenty-five cents that he'd earned and bought a six-pack of Coca-Cola. He split up the bottles and sold them individually from his front yard for a nickel each. "When I sell them all, I clear five cents," he told his mom proudly. Soon, he had a soft-drink stand in his front yard. He eventually found a more profitable venture when he was eleven by selling magazines door-to-door.

When Truett was twelve, two things happened that would affect the rest of his life. The first was that he partnered in a business venture with his brother, Dale. Together, they distributed their own paper route. It was a real business opportunity. For each route, the boys had to find customers, collect payments, and deliver the papers. This was a great learning experience for Truett, and he realized he loved having his brother as his business partner.

Truett made sure that he always treated each paper like he was delivering it to the governor's mansion. He made sure his customers didn't have to dig through the bushes to find it. On rainy days, he delivered it to a dry spot by the front door. He and Dale were a team, eventually earning enough money between them to move the whole family into a new home.

"See, Mom?" he said proudly. "No boarders here."

She gave him a hug. "You're a truly gifted businessman," she said. "Your paper route is just the beginning. One day, you'll have a great business of your own."

The second life-impacting thing that happened when Truett was twelve was that he became a Christian. He had been going to church from a very early age, but at twelve, he made a profound, personal commitment to Jesus Christ as his Savior. His faith began shaping his perspective on life.

His new devotion to Jesus gave him a new love for God's Word. One week in elementary school, every child was asked to bring a Bible verse. The teacher would select a Bible verse for the week and put it on the board. Truett chose Proverbs 22:1 (NKJV), which says, "A good name is to be chosen rather than great riches." That proverb stayed dear to his heart. He considered it as something to live by, and in later years, he had a copy of the verse in his office to remind his employees of its importance.

Truett admittedly wasn't the smartest kid in school. He wasn't the most popular either. In fact, he had little self-confidence and even felt inferior when it came to girls and socializing. But when he read a book called *Think and Grow Rich* by Napoleon Hill, his mindset turned around entirely. "I can do anything, if I want it badly enough," he told himself, and the scene was set for a brighter future.

After high school, both Truett and his brother, Dale, served in the United States Army. They fought bravely for their country during World War II. After the war, Truett was honorably discharged in 1945, at the same time as his brother.

"We've always been a team," Truett said to him. "Let's start a restaurant together."

He already had something in mind: a twenty-four-hour fast-food restaurant serving hamburgers and fries.

"You'll work the first twelve hours, and I'll work the next twelve," he said. The military had helped Truett develop a strong, gritty work ethic.

On Tuesday, May 23, 1946, Truett and Dale Cathy opened the Dwarf Grill in Hapeville, Georgia. The restaurant had only four tables and ten counter stools. They worked so hard staying open twenty-four hours a day that they barely slept their first week. By the time the first Sunday came around, both brothers were extremely exhausted.

"We have to close on Sundays," said Truett. "We need a day of rest. And if we need to rest, the people who work for us are going to need rest too."

Closing on Sundays became one of the cornerstones of Truett Cathy's business. As his company grew, he refused to bow to the pressure to open on Sundays. He needed rest, his people needed rest, and he wanted his employees to have the opportunity to go to church and spend time with their families. He also felt it showed his employees the importance of placing God and family first.

Two years after opening the Dwarf Grill, Truett married Jeannette McNeil, whom he had known since his Sunday school days. When she was young, Jeannette learned the importance of tithing. Following her example, Truett also began to tithe. Truett witnessed firsthand how God blesses a cheerful giver. The Dwarf Grill was becoming more and more successful.

Truett and Dale had great visions of expanding their company. But tragically, in 1949, Dale died in an airplane crash. It was something that Truett couldn't understand. Why would God take his brother, leaving a young wife and child behind? He had no answers.

For the next fourteen years, the Dwarf Grill's business stayed constant with little growth. At one point, Truett considered switching things up to follow the model of Kentucky Fried Chicken, which was doing well. In order to do that, he'd have to be open Sundays, and he was determined to continue to give his employees and himself a weekly day of rest. He had a new idea—and it would be the breakthrough his restaurant needed.

Truett's mother had a unique way of cooking chicken. The way she did it made the chicken incredibly juicy. When a poultry company asked him if he would be interested in buying scraps of chicken from the main product they produced, he agreed. He decided that he was going to create a chicken sandwich that couldn't be beaten.

After trials and testing, Truett was finally ready to introduce his delicious chicken sandwich at the Dwarf Grill. In no time at all, chicken sandwich sales were beating hamburger sales. It was obvious this was a product that could do well for the business. Selling chicken sandwiches rather than hamburgers gave his restaurant a competitive edge that separated his business from competitors. He had finally found his niche in the fast-food industry.

He gave the sandwich the trademarked name of Chick-fil-A and sold the license to different restaurateurs to make the sandwich. Fifty signed up in the first four months, but Truett was worried about the quality. A better long-range plan would be to open different, company-owned restaurants so he could keep control of how the food was prepared.

Early on, Truett had openly incorporated Christianity into his expanding business. He did so by closing on Sundays, but he also put Bible quotes on the Styrofoam cups. In 1982, the year of a significant economic downturn, Truett refused to draw a salary so that his employees wouldn't have to take pay cuts. He believed that Christian principles were good business principles.

Truett Cathy often talked about how important it was to mix business with religion. While business was important to Truett, ministry and serving others was also important. For over fifty years, he was a positive role model to many teens by teaching Sunday school. He always looked for the kid who was lonely or from a broken home and paid extra attention to him.

"It's better to build boys than mend men," he said frequently. These words became the title of a book he wrote.

In the mid-1980s, he founded WinShape Homes, which includes care homes for foster children, retreat getaways, and youth camps. As a company, Chick-fil-A gave $32 million in charitable donations in 2020 alone to groups that fight hunger and homelessness and foster education. The company has continued its founder's legacy of giving.

For Truett, being in the chicken sandwich business was much more about being in the people business. "Nearly every moment of every day we have the opportunity to give something to someone else—our time, our love, our resources," he said. "I have always found more joy in giving when I did not expect anything in return" (Schenk 2014).

Chick-fil-A's purpose statement as a company doesn't include the words *chicken sandwich*. It's a lot greater than that:

> To glorify God by being a faithful steward of all that is entrusted to us. To have a positive influence on all who come in contact with Chick-fil-A. (Chick-Fil-A n.d.)

Honoring God, loving his family, and helping others paid off for Truett Cathy in great ways. His company generated more business in six days than others did in seven—and his employees got to be with their families on Sundays. Chick-fil-A grew to be one of the largest fast-food restaurant chains in America. When he died peacefully in 2014 at the age of ninety-three, he was surrounded by loved ones.

Truett Cathy will be remembered as he wanted to be—a person who knew what his priorities were. "We live in a changing world," he said toward the end of his life. "But we need to be reminded that the important things will not change if we keep our priorities in proper order" (McDaniel 2015, 86).

CONCLUSION

I was blessed by writing *Favor in Business*, and I hope and pray that you have been blessed as well. My purpose in writing was to share how some of the greatest entrepreneurs in American history were tithe-paying, God-fearing businesspeople with a great desire to give and help their neighbors.

In addition to sharing what God put in my heart concerning giving, I also learned so much more about who I am and what my purpose is for God's kingdom. I realized that God uses businesspeople to further His kingdom in the marketplace. It is Christian businesspeople who are a light to people in the marketplace. I have seen how God rewards us when we give, and I can truly say that I've realized we cannot outgive God. When we open our hands to give, we are also opening our hands to receive from the Lord. If we feed and clothe those in need, we are also feeding and clothing Jesus. God will reward our acts of kindness with provision and prosperity.

Thank you for picking up and reading this book. Be blessed and walk in faith. Be in prayer of what God would ask you to do for His kingdom.

Blessings!

REFERENCES

Chapter 1. Anointing with Oil

Gross, Daniel. 1996. *Forbes Greatest Business Stories of All Time.* New York: Byron Preiss Visual Publications.

Kluth, Brian. 2006. "John D. Rockefeller: The First Billionaire." Financial and Generosity Illustrations, Stories, Humor & Quotes. www.kluth.org.

Meah, Asad. 2017. "30 Inspirational John D. Rockefeller Quotes on Success." Awaken the Greatness Within. Accessed March 2020. https://www.awakenthegreatnesswithin.com/30-inspirational-john-d-rockefeller-quotes-success.

Mike. 2018. "Why John D. Rockefeller Could Teach Christian Millionaires." God Interest. https://godinterest.com/2018/06/09/why-john-d-rockefeller-could-teach-christian-millionaires.

Rockefeller, John, Sr. 2006. "Yes I Tithe." Stories & Testimonies. Accessed October 2020. http://www.wrcog.net/silver_treasures13.html.

Segall, Grant. 2001. *John D. Rockefeller: Anointed with Oil.* Oxford, United Kingdom: Oxford University Press.

Tan, Paul Lee. 1998. *Encyclopedia of 15,000 Illustrations.* From a sermon by Scott Walker, "The Good and Beautiful God: God is Holy."

Chapter 2. Cleanliness Is Godliness

Brott, Rich. 2007. "Business People Who Gave Generously." Rich Brott. http://www.richbrott.com/wp-content/uploads/2007/08/business-people-who-gave-generously.pdf.

Colgate-Palmolive. n.d. "Our Commitment to Our Communities." https://www.colgatepalmolive.com/en-us/core-values/community-responsibility.

Hansell, George H. 1899. "Deacon William Colgate." Baptist History Homepage. Accessed May 2020. http://baptisthistoryhomepage. com/ny.colgate.wm.bio.html.

Reformed Reader. n.d. "William Colgate." http://www.reformedreader.org/ colgate.htm.

Chapter 3. Ketchup Empire

Astrum People. n.d. "Henry J. Heinz Biography: Success Story of Heinz Ketchup Empire." https://astrumpeople.com/henry-j-heinz-biography.

Carnegie Medal of Philanthropy. 2022. "The Heinz Family: Many Varieties of Giving." https://www.medalofphilanthropy.org/profiles-in-philan thropic-courage-the-heinz-family.

Gliozzi, Diane. 2015. "H. J. Heinz: A Pittsburgh Legacy." Popular Pittsburgh. https://popularpittsburgh.com/heinz-legacy.

Leigh, Silvia. 2013. "Henry J. Heinz (1844–1919)." Father's Call. https:// fatherscall.com/2013/05/16/henry-j-heinz-1844-1919.

Lukas, Paul. 2003. "H. J. Heinz at a time when prepared food was a shady business, Heinz's transparent jars, factory tours, and focus on food safety made his store-bought condiments king." *Money*, CNN. Accessed March 2020. https://money.cnn.com/magazines/fsb/fsb_ archive/2003/04/01/341007.

Richardson, William E. 2012. "Henry Heinz." Lights 4 God. https:// lights4god.wordpress.com/2012/10/11/henry-heinz.

Chapter 4. It's the Real Thing

Adams, Ann Uhry. 2012. *Formula for Fortune: How Asa Candler Discovered Coca-Cola and Turned it Into the Wealth His Children Enjoyed.* Bloomington, Indiana: iUniverse.

Coca-Cola Company. n.d. "The Asa Candler Era—Coca-Cola History." https://www.coca-colacompany.com/company/history/the-asa-candler-era.

Editors of Encyclopedia Britannica. 1998. "Asa Griggs Candler-American Manufacturer." https://www.britannica.com/biography/ Asa-Griggs-Candler.

Kemp, Kathryn. 2002. "Asa Candler: 1851–1929." Georgia Encyclopedia. https://www.georgiaencyclopedia.org/articles/history-archaeology/asa-candler-1851-1929.

Kemp, Kathryn. 2002. *God's Capitalist: Asa Candler of Coca-Cola*. Macon, GA: Mercer University Press.

Reference. 2016. "Asa Griggs Candler." https://reference.jrank.org/biography-2/Candler_Asa_Griggs.html.

Wikipedia. n.d. "Asa Griggs Candler." https://en.wikipedia.org/wiki/Asa_Griggs_Candler.

Chapter 5. Nothing Is Better for Thee than Me

Challies, Tim. 2013. "The Philanthropists: Henry Crowell." Challies. https://www.challies.com/articles/the-philanthropists-henry-crowell.

Crowell Trust. n.d. "About Us." http://crowelltrust.org/about-us.

Giants for God. 2010. "Henry Parsons Crowell." http://www.giantsforgod.com/henry-parsons-crowell-quaker-oats.

Johnson, Laura. 2013. "Spreading the Word: Henry Parsons Crowell, Mass Media, and the Moody Bible Institute." Research Gate. https://www.researchgate.net/publication/267884212_Spreading_the_Word_Henry_Parsons_Crowell_Mass_Media_and_the_Moody_Bible_Institute.

Quaker Oats. n.d. "Our Oat Origins." https://www.quakeroats.com/about-quaker-oats/content/quaker-history.aspx.

Scalar. 2016. "The Honorable Mentions of the Breakfast Cereal Revolution." http://scalar.usc.edu/works/early-years-of-ready-to-eat-breakfast-cereal/the-smaller-players-in-the-breakfast-cereal-revolution.

Wikipedia. n.d. "Crowell Trust." https://en.wikipedia.org/wiki/Crowell_Trust.

Wikipedia. n.d. "Henry Parsons Crowell." https://en.wikipedia.org/wiki/Henry_Parsons_Crowell.

Chapter 6. There's a Smile in Every Hershey's Bar

Biography.com editors. 2019. "Milton Hershey Biography." Biography. https://www.biography.com/people/milton-hershey-9337133.

Civello Photo. 2010. "Inside Hershey: 100 Sweet Facts about Hershey." http://civellophoto.typepad.com/hersheyinsider/2010/09/100-sweet-facts-about-hershey-milton-s-hershey.html.

Hershey Archives. n.d. "Hershey Archives." https://hersheyarchives.org.

Hershey Story. n.d. "Who Was Milton S. Hershey?" https://hersheystory.org/milton-hershey-history/

MHS Kids. n.d. "Milton Hershey School History." https://www.mhskids.org/about/school-history/milton-s-hershey.

Prabook. n.d. "Milton Snavely Hershey." https://prabook.com/web/milton.hershey/730028.

Shell, Adam, and Nicholas Kraft. Jan. 9, 2014. "Happiness is Chocolate." Live Happy. https://www.livehappy.com/happiness-is-chocolate.

Sprout, Jonathan. 2009. "Milton Snavely Hershey." Jon Sprout. http://www.jonsprout.com/cms/index.php/my-heroes/42-milton-hershey.

Chapter 7. A Little Taste of Heaven

Entrepreneurs Here and There. 2013. "James L. Kraft." https://sites.google.com/site/wmcientrepreneurs/entrepreneurs-from-away/james-l-kraft.

History of Business. n.d. "Kraft Foods." http://historyofbusiness.blogspot.com.au/2009/06/kraft-foods.html.

Joy Christian Ministries. 2015. "Doing It Right!" We Are Joy. https://www.wearejoy.church/from-the-heart-of-jc/doing-it-right.

LaMattina, Chuck. 2011. "Kraft Cheese and Tithing." Essential Matters. http://essentialmatters.blogspot.com.au/2011/11/kraft-cheese-and-tithing.html.

Mink, Michael. 2014. "James Kraft Cooked Up a New Cheese and a New Market." Investors. https://www.investors.com/news/management/leaders-and-success/james-kraft-founded-kraft-cheese.

Mullen, Michael, and Lynne Galia. 2020. "Kraft Heinz Commits $12 Million." Business Wire. https://www.businesswire.com/news/home/20200320005358/en/Kraft-Heinz-Commits-12-Million-Globally-in-Support-of-Communities-Impacted-By-COVID-19-Outbreak.

Rhoads, Mark. 2006. "Illinois Hall of Fame: James L. Kraft." *Illinois Review.* http://illinoisreview.typepad.com/illinoisreview/2006/11/illinois_hall_o_7.html.

Sponholtz, Lloyd L. 2000. "Kraft, James Lewis." American National Biography. https://www.anb.org/view/10.1093/anb/9780198606697.001.0001/anb-9780198606697-e-1000942.

Chapter 8. Every Day Matters

Gross, Daniel. 1996. *Forbes Greatest Business Stories of All Time.* New York: Byron Preiss Visual Publications.

Plumb, Beatrice. 1963. *J. C. Penney: Merchant Prince.* Minneapolis, T. S. Denison & Company Publishers.

Tibbetts, Orlando L. 1999. *The Spiritual Journey of J. C. Penney.* Netsource Dist Services.

Chapter 9. Pure Squeezed Sunshine

Aurora Ministries. n.d. "Our History." https://www.auroraministries.org/pages/about-u.

Christian Business Daily. 2007. "Anthony Rossi—Founder of Tropicana." https://christianbusinessnetwork.com/resources/wisdom-at-work/entry/anthony-rossi.

Florida Citrus Hall of Fame. n.d. "Anthony T. Rossi." https://floridacitrushalloffame.com/inductees/anthony-t-rossi.

Funding Universe. n.d. "Tropicana Products, Inc. History." http://www.fundinguniverse.com/company-histories/tropicana-products-inc-history.

Giants for God. 2016. "Anthony Rossi—Tropicana." http://www.giantsforgod.com/anthony-rossi-tropicana.

LA Times. 1993. "Anthony T. Rossi; Founder of Tropicana Products." https://www.latimes.com/archives/la-xpm-1993-01-28-mn-2221-story.html.

Rossi, Sanna Barlow. 1986. *Anthony T. Rossi Christian & Entrepreneur: The Story of the Founder of Tropicana.* InterVarsity Press.

Wikipedia. n.d. "1908 Messina Earthquake." https://en.wikipedia.org/wiki/1908_Messina_earthquake.

Chapter 10. Save Money—Live Better

Gross, Daniel. 1996. *Forbes Greatest Business Stories of All Time.* New York: Byron Preiss Visual Publications.

Walton Family Foundation. n.d. "About Us." https://www.waltonfamilyfoundation.org/about-us.

Walton, Sam. 1992. *Made in America.* New York: Doubleday Dell Publishing Group.

Chapter 11. If You Think You Can, You Can

Ash, Mary Kay. "Celebrating Mary Kay Ash." Mary Kay. www.marykaytribute.com.

Gross, Daniel. 1996. *Forbes Greatest Business Stories of All Time.* New York: Byron Preiss Visual Publications.

Mary Kay Tribute. n.d. "Her Wisdom- Faith." http://www.marykaytribute.com/wisdomfaith.aspx.

Miller, Calvin. 1989. *A Requiem for Love.* W. Pub Group.

Prabook. n.d. "Mary Kay Ash." https://prabook.com/web/mary.ash/3734856.

Chapter 12. Eat Mor Chikin

Bhasin, Kim. 2012. "Meet S. Truett Cathy, The 91-Year-Old Billionaire Behind Chick-fil-A." Business Insider. https://www.businessinsider.com.au/meet-chick-fil-a-founder-s-truett-cathy-2012-7#OzdtuaTVm3c8Hzxd.99.

Cathy, Truett. 2004. *It's Better to Build Boys than Mend Men.* Chicago, IL: Looking Glass Books, Inc.

Chick-fil-A. n.d. "Company History." https://www.chick-fil-a.com/About/History.

Chick-Fil-A. n.d. "Our Purpose." https://www.chick-fil-a.com/careers/culture.

Daszkowski, Don. 2019. "The Story of S. Truett Cathy." The Balance. https://www.thebalance.com/s-truett-cathy-bio-chick-fil-a-story-1350972.

Forbes. 2014. "#224 S. Truett Cathy." https://www.forbes.com/profile/s-truett-cathy.

Giants for God. 2013. "S. Truett Cathy- Chick-fil-A." http://www.giantsforgod.com/s-truett-cathy.

Green, Emma. 2014. "Chick-fil-A: Selling Chicken with a Side of God." The *Atlantic.* https://www.theatlantic.com/business/archive/2014/09/chick-fil-a-selling-chicken-with-a-side-of-god/379776.

Jones, Russ. 2014. "5 Things Christians Need to Know about Chick-fil-A Founder Truett Cathy." *Christian Press.* https://www.christianheadlines.com/news/5-things-christians-need-to-know-about-chick-fil-a-founder-truett-cathy.html.

McDaniel, Phyllis G. 2015. *Don't Lose Faith: Keep Believing.* Lulu.com.

Ohlheiser, Abby. 2014. "The World According to Chick-fil-A Founder Truett Cathy." *Washington Post*. https://www.washingtonpost.com/news/morning-mix/wp/2014/09/08/the-world-according-to-chick-fil-a-founder-truett-cathy/?utm_term=.fbc6dd2ad7ec.

Parker, Dick. 2016. "A Life Centered on Family." The Chicken Wire. https://thechickenwire.chick-fil-a.com/Inside-Chick-fil-A/A-Life-Centered-on-Family.

Parker, Dick. 2016. "Humble Beginnings." The Chicken Wire. https://thechickenwire.chick-fil-a.com/Inside-Chick-fil-A/Humble-Beginnings-How-Truett-Cathys-Love-for-Customers-Grew-From-a-Coke-and-Smile.

Ramsey Solutions. 2021. "7 Life Lessons from Truett Cathy." Ramsey Solutions. https://www.daveramsey.com/blog/7-life-lessons-from-truett-cathy.

Schenk, Ruth. 2014. "Chick-Fil-A Founder, Truett Cathy, Leaves a Godly Legacy." The *Southeast Outlook*. http://www.southeastoutlook.org/news/features/article_9266b69c-38f4-11e4-9433-0017a43b2370.html.

Warren, Rick. 2014. "Chick-fil-A Founder Truett Cathy Truly Lived His Faith." *Time*. http://time.com/3310038/rick-warren-chick-fil-a-founder-truett-cathy-truly-lived-his-faith.

Printed in the United States
by Baker & Taylor Publisher Services